DAY HIKES IN THE
BEARTOOTH
MOUNTAINS

RED LODGE, MONTANA TO
YELLOWSTONE NATIONAL PARK

by Robert Stone

Day Hike Books, Inc.
RED LODGE, MONTANA

Published by Day Hike Books, Inc.
P.O. Box 865
Red Lodge, Montana 59068

Distributed by The Globe Pequot Press
246 Goose Lane
P.O. Box 480
Guilford, CT 06437-0480
800-243-0495 (direct order) · 800-820-2329 (fax order)
www.globe-pequot.com

Photographs by Robert Stone
Design by Paula Doherty

The author has made every attempt to provide accurate
information in this book. However, trail routes and features may
change—please use common sense and forethought, and be mindful
of your own capabilities. Let this book guide you, but be aware
that each hiker assumes responsibility for their own safety.
The author and publisher do not assume any responsibility for loss,
damage or injury caused through the use of this book.

Cover photo: Clarks Fork Canyon Falls—Hikes 44—47
Back cover photo: Sheep Creek Falls—Hikes 52

Table of Contents

THE HIKES

Stillwater, West Rosebud, East Rosebud and Luther

West Fork

Main Fork and Lake Fork of Rock Creek

The Beartooth Plateau and Beartooth Highway

Around Cooke City, Silver Gate
and Yellowstone National Park

About the Hikes

The Beartooth Mountains are a beautiful rugged range that lie in south-central Montana and northern Wyoming, bordering Yellowstone National Park. Weaving throughout these mountains and the foothills are an extensive network of hiking trails. This guide will take you to 58 of the best day hikes in the Beartooth Range and along the Beartooth Highway.

Nearly every hiking trail in the area is covered. Hikes range from easy to strenuous and from short to full-day. The trails have been chosen for their scenery, variety and ability to be hiked within a day. To help you decide which hikes are most appealing to you, a brief summary of the highlights is included with each hike. The hikes are also accompanied with their own maps and detailed driving and hiking directions. You may enjoy these areas for a short time or the whole day.

All trailheads are located within a 75-mile radius of Red Lodge. The hikes lie along the Beartooth Front from the Stillwater River drainage to Red Lodge and from Red Lodge to Yellowstone National Park. (See overall map on next page.) The hikes travel into picturesque drainages and canyons of the Beartooth Range and across the Beartooth Highway, the mountain pass connecting Red Lodge to the park.

The Beartooth Highway is the major access road to many of the hikes in this book. This dramatic highway (Highway 212) begins in Red Lodge, passes through the towns of Cooke City and Silver Gate, and extends to the northeast entrance of Yellowstone Park. The famous switchbacks start along the east wall of Rock Creek Canyon at 6,000 feet and quickly rise to a top-of-the-world elevation of 10,947 feet. The views from this area are spectacular.

The 68-mile Beartooth Highway was originally built in 1936. It has since been designated a National Scenic Byway and heralded as "the most scenic highway in America" by Charles Kuralt of CBS News. Although the highway starts and ends in Montana, it crosses into Wyoming along the way. The highway is open, weather permitting, Memorial Day through mid-October.

The three-billion-year-old Beartooth Mountains, which include the Gallatin, Custer and Shoshone National Forests, surround the Beartooth Highway. These ancient mountains are among the oldest rocks on earth and lie within a 945,000-acre protected wilderness area. The Beartooth Plateau, shaped by alpine glaciers, is the largest continuous area above 10,000 feet and the largest alpine tundra region in North America. This rugged, majestic mountain range contains glaciers, deep canyons, streams, waterfalls, over a thousand lakes, vast alpine meadows, lush forests, panoramic views and abundant wildlife. Hikers will discover the diverse and scenic alpine landscape of the Beartooth Mountains, Montana's highest mountain range.

This guide is designed for the day hiker who wants a concise but easy reference to the area's best trails and their features. To extend your hike into the backcountry, the trails are also detailed on an assortment of commercial maps. These include the Rocky Mountain Survey maps, U.S. Geological Survey topographical maps and national forest maps produced by the Forest Service. Relevant maps are listed with each hike and can be purchased at several locations in Red Lodge.

Be sure to dress appropriately for your hike. The elevation may be nearly 11,000 feet on the alpine plateaus. The air is usually cool and weather often changes abruptly. Be prepared for unpredictable weather by wearing layered clothing and packing a rain coat, hat and gloves. Wear supportive, comfortable hiking shoes. A snack and drinking water are a must for the longer hikes. Both black and grizzly bears inhabit the region, so wear a bear bell and hike in a group whenever possible.

Hiking in the Beartooth Mountains will give you a deeper appreciation of the beauty of this region, whether you live here year-round or are only passing through. Enjoy your day hike as you discover the Beartooth Mountain backcountry!

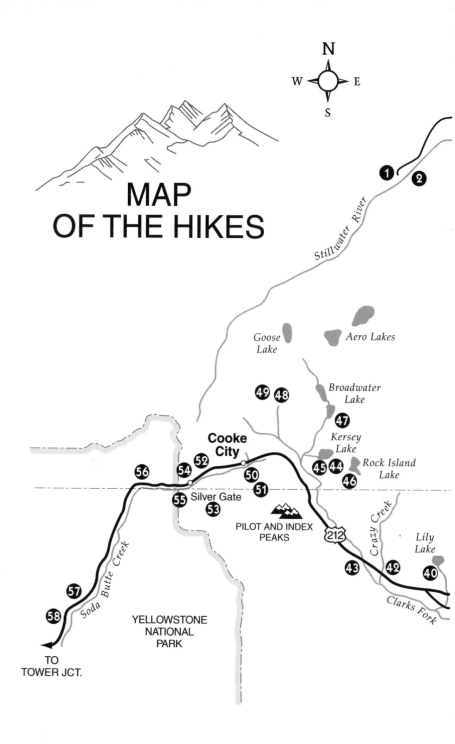

MAP
OF THE HIKES

Stillwater River

Goose Lake

Aero Lakes

Broadwater Lake

49 48

Kersey Lake

47

Cooke City

Rock Island Lake

56 54 52

50

45 44

46

55 Silver Gate

51

53

PILOT AND INDEX
PEAKS

212

Crazy Creek

Lily Lake

43

42

40

Clarks Fork

57

Soda Butte Creek

58

YELLOWSTONE
NATIONAL
PARK

TO
TOWER JCT.

1 2

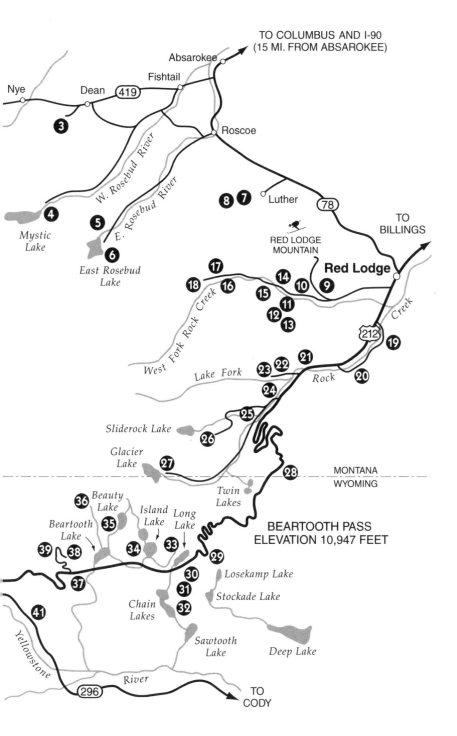

TO COLUMBUS AND I-90
(15 MI. FROM ABSAROKEE)

Absarokee

Fishtail

Nye

Dean ⑷⁹

❸

Roscoe

W. Rosebud River

E. Rosebud River

❹

Mystic
Lake

❺

❻

East Rosebud
Lake

❽❼ Luther

⑺⁸

TO
BILLINGS

RED LODGE
MOUNTAIN

Red Lodge

⑰

⑱ ⑯

⑭

⑩ ❾

⑮

⑪

⑫ ⑬

West Fork Rock Creek

Lake Fork

Rock

Creek

②¹²

⑲

㉓ ㉒ ㉑

㉔

⑳

Sliderock Lake

㉕

㉖

Glacier
Lake

㉗

㉘

MONTANA
WYOMING

Twin
Lakes

㊱ Beauty
Lake

㉟

Island
Lake

Long
Lake

BEARTOOTH PASS
ELEVATION 10,947 FEET

Beartooth
Lake

㉞

㉝

㊴ ㊳

㉙

㊲

㉚ Losekamp Lake

㉛

Stockade Lake

㉜

㊶

Chain
Lakes

Sawtooth
Lake

Deep Lake

Yellowstone

River

²⁹⁶

TO
CODY

Fifty-eight Great Hikes - **9**

Hike 1
Sioux Charley Lake

Hiking distance: 6 miles round trip
Hiking time: 3 hours
Elevation gain: 600 feet
Maps: R.M.S. Mt. Wood
       U.S.G.S. Cathedral Point

Summary of hike: The hike to Sioux Charley Lake follows the Stillwater River through a narrow, steep-walled canyon and across a wide, pristine valley surrounded by majestic mountains. Throughout the hike, the Stillwater River puts on a dynamic display of waterfalls, cascades and rapids as the river rages down the drainage. Sioux Charley Lake is a long, wide, slow-moving section of the Stillwater River.

Driving directions: From the north end of Red Lodge, drive 30 miles west on Highway 78 to County Road 419, the Fishtail and Nye turnoff on the left. Turn left and continue 28.3 miles to a road fork. Take the right fork 0.4 miles to the parking area.

Hiking directions: The trail heads south from the far end of the parking area and follows the Stillwater River upstream along its north bank. Within minutes the trail enters a steep-walled gorge with swiftly tumbling whitewater. At 0.5 miles, the trail leaves the gorge and enters into a valley meadow. The trail moderately gains elevation through the valley. The trail then curves north to a rocky knoll. From this overlook are views of the Stillwater drainage and the north end of Sioux Charley Lake. Across the valley to the east, the burn area from the 1988 Storm Creek fire can be seen. From here, the trail descends through the meadow past aspen groves and crosses a series of streams to Sioux Charley Lake. This is our turnaround spot.

To hike further, the trail continues for many miles parallel to the Stillwater River to its headwaters near Cooke City.

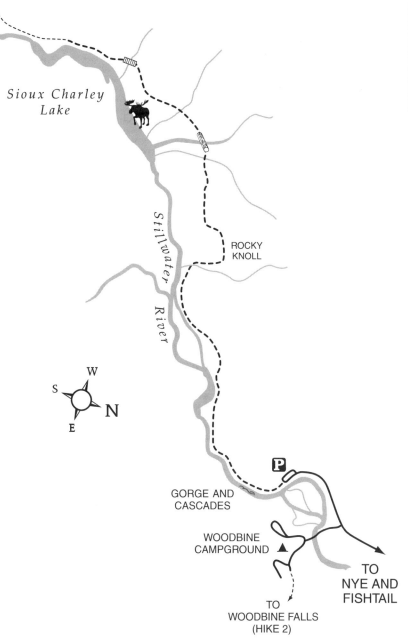

Sioux Charley Lake

Stillwater River

ROCKY
KNOLL

W
S
N
E

P

GORGE AND
CASCADES

WOODBINE
CAMPGROUND ▲

TO
WOODBINE FALLS
(HIKE 2)

TO
NYE AND
FISHTAIL

SIOUX CHARLEY LAKE

Hike 2
Woodbine Falls

Hiking distance: 1.5 miles round trip
Hiking time: 1 hour
Elevation gain: 300 feet
Maps: R.M.S. Mt. Wood
U.S.G.S. Cathedral Point
U.S.F.S. Absaroka-Beartooth Wilderness

Summary of hike: Woodbine Falls is a long, stunning free-falling waterfall located a short distance from the trailhead. The trail leads to a lookout and stays close to the frothy, cascading whitewater of Woodbine Creek.

Driving directions: From the north end of Red Lodge, drive 30 miles west on Highway 78 to County Road 419, the Fishtail and Nye turnoff on the left. Turn left and continue 28.3 miles to a road fork, located 3 miles beyond the Stillwater Mine. Take the left fork 0.4 miles into Woodbine Campground, bearing left at a junction, to the trailhead parking area on the left.

Hiking directions: Hike past the trailhead sign to Woodbine Creek. Head upstream to the footbridge. After crossing the bridge, the trail begins a series of gentle switchbacks through the forest. The trail stays close to the raging whitewater of Woodbine Creek. At 0.4 miles, the trail enters the Absaroka-Beartooth Wilderness. The trail crosses small tributaries with lush, mossy alcoves along the mountain side. At 0.75 miles is the Woodbine Falls lookout, corralled by a curved rock wall. This is our turnaround spot.

Just before reaching the lookout, a steep, unmaintained trail leads to the left up to the brink of the falls. Although this trail is frequently hiked, this portion of the trail has loose rock and gravel and is not recommended. The trail is especially dangerous coming down.

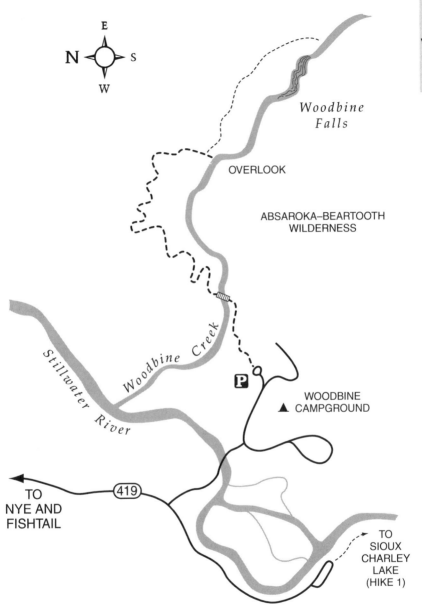

Woodbine Falls

OVERLOOK

ABSAROKA–BEARTOOTH
WILDERNESS

Stillwater River

Woodbine Creek

P

WOODBINE
▲ CAMPGROUND

419

TO
NYE AND
FISHTAIL

TO
SIOUX
CHARLEY
LAKE
(HIKE 1)

WOODBINE FALLS

Hike 3
Benbow Jeep Road—East Fishtail Creek Trail to Island Lake and Twin Lakes

Hiking distance: 8 miles round trip
Hiking time: 4 hours
Elevation gain: 800 feet
Maps: U.S.G.S. Beehive and Emerald Lake
      U.S.F.S. Absaroka Beartooth Wilderness

Summary of hike: This diverse and scenic hike crosses open meadows, passes through aspen and pine forests, and fords streams and creeks on its way to Island Lake and Twin Lakes. There is an overlook of the majestic Beartooth Mountain Range. The lakes, part of the West Rosebud Creek system, are located near the small town of Dean.

Driving directions: From the north end of Red Lodge, drive 30 miles west on Highway 78 to County Road 419, the Fishtail and Nye turnoff on the left. Turn left and continue 13.9 miles to Benbow Road at the west end of Dean. Turn left and drive 2.3 miles to the unpaved road on the left marked "Pole Unit Firewood Area," 0.5 miles past the Custer National Forest sign. Turn left and park just ahead on the wide, flat area on the right.

Hiking directions: Walk up the jeep road through open forest, reaching the Benbow Jeep Road/East Fishtail Trail #37 sign at a quarter mile. Continue through aspen groves and a new-growth fir forest. At 0.8 miles, cross through a cattle fence and cross the plateau to a saddle. Descend into the forested drainage to a junction and trail sign at 1.2 miles. Stay on the jeep road, curving to the right and heading uphill to the ridge. The road levels out to a signed trail junction at just under 2 miles. Leave the road and take the footpath to the left, descending to an overlook of the Beartooth Front. Continue downhill to the Rickman-Kennedy Ditch at 2.5 miles. Cross over the log to a trail split, the beginning of the loop. Begin the loop on the left fork. In a half mile, the path skirts the west edge of North Twin Lake.

Follow a water flume from Twin Lakes to Island Lake, reaching the inlet cascade at Island Lake. After exploring the lake, return to the inlet stream and make a short, steep descent on the main trail along the cascading stream. After crossing, follow the hillside through a ponderosa pine forest. Watch for a "Please Close Gate" sign. (For an extended hike, this detour through the gate crosses West Fishtail Creek to a creekside stroll along East Fishtail Creek.) Back on the main trail, pass through another gate. Ford the creek, completing the loop. Return by retracing your steps.

East Fishtail Creek

West Fishtail Creek

Twin Lakes

Island Lake

Rickman-Kennedy Ditch

TO BENBOW MINE

TO BENBOW MINE

S
E — W
N

CUSTER NATIONAL FOREST

BENBOW ROAD

TO BENBOW MINE

P

Dean

TO HWY 78

(419)

TO HIKES 1 AND 2

BENBOW JEEP ROAD

Hike 4
Mystic Lake

Hiking distance: 7 miles round trip
Hiking time: 3.5 hours
Elevation gain: 1,200 feet
Maps: R.M.S. Alpine-Cooke City
U.S.G.S. Alpine and Granite Peak

Summary of hike: Mystic Lake is the largest lake in the Beartooths, covering more than 430 acres. It is a natural lake with a hydro-electric dam at the east end. The hike to Mystic Lake follows the West Rosebud Trail uphill for 1,200 feet. The hike offers spectacular views of the West Rosebud Valley, including Emerald and West Rosebud Lakes. From the top are beautiful views of Mystic Lake, West Rosebud Canyon and the surrounding mountain peaks.

Driving directions: From the north end of Red Lodge, drive 30 miles west on Highway 78 to County Road 419, the Fishtail and Nye turnoff on the left. Turn left and continue 4.3 miles to the West Rosebud Road on the left. Turn left and drive 6.4 miles to a road split. Take the left fork, and drive 14 miles to the trailhead parking area on the left at the end of the road.

Hiking directions: From the parking area, continue up the road past the power plant and a few houses to the trailhead sign. Cross the wooden bridge over the railroad tracks to the footpath. The trail heads upstream along West Rosebud Creek. At 0.75 miles, the trail crosses a wooden footbridge to the south side of the creek. A short distance after crossing, the trail enters the Absaroka-Beartooth Wilderness. The trail continues uphill. There are a series of switchbacks through rock fields as you near the top. Once over the ridge, there are views of Mystic Lake and the dam. The trail descends to the east shore of the lake and a sandy beach. The trail levels and follows the south shore of the lake to a junction with the Phantom Creek Trail, which leads to the East Rosebud drainage. This is the turn-

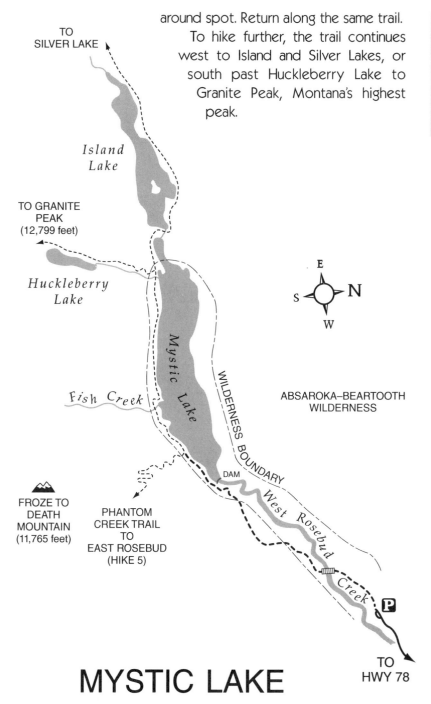

around spot. Return along the same trail. To hike further, the trail continues west to Island and Silver Lakes, or south past Huckleberry Lake to Granite Peak, Montana's highest peak.

TO
SILVER LAKE

*Island
Lake*

TO GRANITE
PEAK
(12,799 feet)

*Huckleberry
Lake*

Mystic Lake

Fish Creek

WILDERNESS BOUNDARY

E
N
S
W

ABSAROKA–BEARTOOTH
WILDERNESS

DAM

West Rosebud

Creek

FROZE TO
DEATH
MOUNTAIN
(11,765 feet)

PHANTOM
CREEK TRAIL
TO
EAST ROSEBUD
(HIKE 5)

P

TO
HWY 78

MYSTIC LAKE

Hike 5
Phantom Creek Trail
to Slough Lake

Hiking distance: 5 miles round trip
Hiking time: 2.5 hours
Elevation gain: 1,200 feet
Maps: R.M.S. Alpine-Cooke City
U.S.G.S. Alpine

Summary of hike: The Phantom Creek Trail is one of two primary routes used to reach 12,799-foot Granite Peak, the highest peak in Montana. This hike takes in the first 2.5 miles of the trail to Slough Lake, paralleling Armstrong Creek. (Beyond Slough Lake, the creek is named Phantom Creek.) Slough Lake is actually two wide spots of the creek. The lake is in a large, glacier-carved meadow surrounded by imposing mountain peaks.

Driving directions: From the north end of Red Lodge, drive 20 miles west on Highway 78 to the town of Roscoe, and turn left on the East Rosebud Road. Continue 13.5 miles to the Phantom Creek trailhead parking area on the right. It is located 0.4 miles before reaching East Rosebud Lake.

Hiking directions: From the parking area, the trail heads west. A series of gradual switchbacks lead into the Absaroka-Beartooth Wilderness, with views south of East Rosebud Lake. The trail hugs the north wall of the canyon above the tumbling Armstrong Creek. Continue uphill past two boulder fields and numerous streams. At two miles, the trail begins to level out. As you approach Slough Lake, the canyon opens to a large meadow surrounded by mountains. The trail follows the north edge of Slough Lake and the meadow. This is our turnaround spot. Return along the same trail.

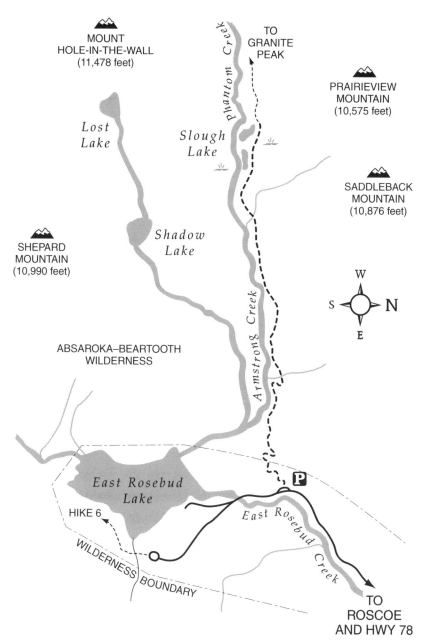

MOUNT
HOLE-IN-THE-WALL
(11,478 feet)

Lost
Lake

Phantom Creek

TO
GRANITE
PEAK

PRAIRIEVIEW
MOUNTAIN
(10,575 feet)

Slough
Lake

SADDLEBACK
MOUNTAIN
(10,876 feet)

Shadow
Lake

SHEPARD
MOUNTAIN
(10,990 feet)

Armstrong Creek

W

S ◇ N

E

ABSAROKA–BEARTOOTH
WILDERNESS

East Rosebud
Lake

HIKE 6

East Rosebud Creek

WILDERNESS BOUNDARY

P

TO
ROSCOE
AND HWY 78

PHANTOM CREEK TRAIL

Hike 6
East Rosebud Trail
to Elk Lake

Hiking distance: 6 miles round trip
Hiking time: 3 hours
Elevation gain: 500 feet
Maps: R.M.S. Alpine-Cooke City
       U.S.G.S. Alpine

Summary of hike: The East Rosebud Trail is a popular 26-mile hiking and horsepacking trail to Cooke City. This hike takes in the first three miles up the East Rosebud Canyon to Elk Lake, a seven-acre lake surrounded by mountain peaks. The trail parallels East Rosebud Creek, passing a 50-foot waterfall along the way. Part of the trail winds through the burn area from the 1996 fires. There are superb views of Shepard Mountain to the west and Sylvan Peak to the east.

Driving directions: From the north end of Red Lodge, drive 20 miles west on Highway 78 to the town of Roscoe, and turn left on the East Rosebud Road. Continue 14.4 miles to the East Rosebud trailhead parking area at the end of the road on the east side of East Rosebud Lake.

Hiking directions: From the parking area, hike south past the trailhead sign along the east side of the lake. Rock hop across an inlet stream near the south end of the lake. The trail climbs to an overlook of the lake and East Rosebud Creek. Begin a short descent into the majestic canyon, entering the Absaroka-Beartooth Wilderness. The trail heads up canyon, overlooking the tumbling whitewater of the creek. A series of switchbacks lead past a waterfall at 1.2 miles. Cross several streams, including a wooden bridge over Snow Creek where another waterfall can be seen dropping off the cliffs high above. The trail enters the forest, then arrives at Elk Lake. Return by retracing your steps.

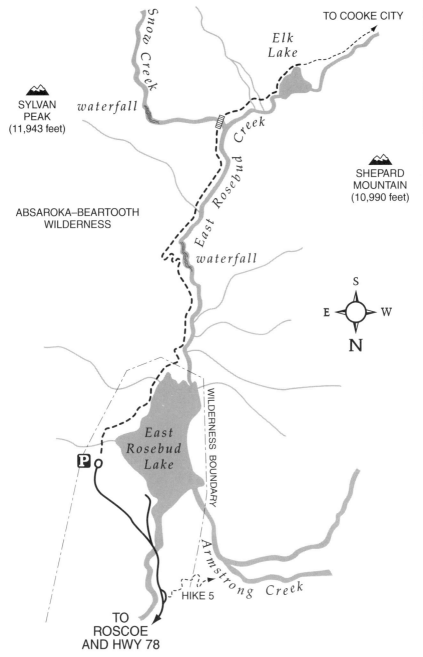

TO COOKE CITY

Elk
Lake

Snow Creek

waterfall

SYLVAN
PEAK
(11,943 feet)

East Rosebud Creek

SHEPARD
MOUNTAIN
(10,990 feet)

ABSAROKA–BEARTOOTH
WILDERNESS

waterfall

S
E W
N

WILDERNESS BOUNDARY

East
Rosebud
Lake

P

Armstrong Creek

HIKE 5

TO
ROSCOE
AND HWY 78

EAST ROSEBUD TRAIL

Hike 7
West Red Lodge Creek Trail
to Wilderness Boundary

Hiking distance: 2.5 miles round trip
Hiking time: 1.5 hours
Elevation gain: 600 feet
Maps: R.M.S. Alpine-Mount Maurice
U.S.G.S. Bare Mountain and Sylvan Peak

Summary of hike: The West Red Lodge Creek Trail begins near the town of Luther and climbs strenuously up to the Red Lodge Creek Plateau and Crow Lake (Hike 8). This hike follows the easier first portion of the trail in the foothills along West Red Lodge Creek. The trail leads to the mouth of a narrow rock canyon and a log bridge at the wilderness boundary.

Driving directions: From Red Lodge, drive 12.7 miles north-west on Highway 78 to the Luther Lower Road, the second Luther turnoff between mile markers 12 and 13. Turn left and drive 2.4 miles to a T-junction in the town of Luther. Turn right on the Luther/Roscoe Road, and go 0.5 miles to Red Lodge Creek Road. Turn left and continue 2.6 miles to the signed Custer National Forest boundary and a road split. Take the right fork on Forest Service Road 2141, and drive 1.3 miles to a signed trailhead parking area on the right.

Hiking directions: Head southwest across the open flat toward the forest. The near-level path parallels West Red Lodge Creek across trickling streams and water ditches to an old road at 0.8 miles. Bear left, staying close to the creek, toward the jagged outcroppings. Curve left into the mouth of the canyon drainage. Pass huge mossy boulders to a log bridge and cascading creek at the Absaroka-Beartooth Wilderness boundary. Cross the bridge and continue a short distance up the rock-walled canyon to a second creek crossing which you must wade across. This is our turnaround spot. To hike to the top of Red Lodge Creek Plateau, continue with the next hike.

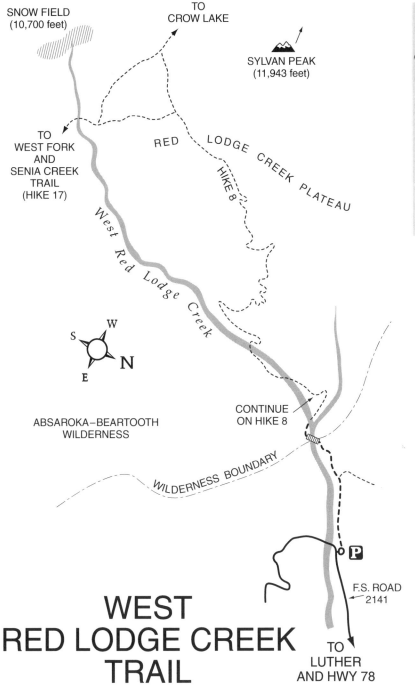

SNOW FIELD
(10,700 feet)

TO
CROW LAKE

SYLVAN PEAK
(11,943 feet)

TO
WEST FORK
AND
SENIA CREEK
TRAIL
(HIKE 17)

RED   LODGE   CREEK PLATEAU

HIKE 8

West Red Lodge Creek

W
S   N
E

ABSAROKA–BEARTOOTH
WILDERNESS

CONTINUE
ON HIKE 8

WILDERNESS BOUNDARY

P

F.S. ROAD
2141

WEST
RED LODGE CREEK
TRAIL

TO
LUTHER
AND HWY 78

Hike 8
West Red Lodge Creek Trail
to Red Lodge Creek Plateau

Hiking distance: 14 miles round trip (or 12-mile shuttle)
Hiking time: 8 hours
Elevation gain: 4,000 feet
Maps: R.M.S. Alpine-Mount Maurice
       U.S.G.S. Bare Mountain and Sylvan Peak

Summary of hike: The West Red Lodge Creek Trail begins near the town of Luther and climbs to the Red Lodge Creek Plateau and Crow Lake. It is a full-day strenuous hike to this alpine plateau. There are great views of Sylvan Peak, Bare Mountain and the Silver Run Plateau. This steep trail can be hiked as a 12-mile shuttle hike with the Senia Creek Trail (Hike 17).

Driving directions: Follow the driving directions for Hike 7.

Hiking directions: From the bridge crossing over West Red Lodge Creek at the wilderness boundary—where hike 7 leaves off—continue along the south side of the creek up the narrow canyon. Pass towering rock walls and jagged spires. Wade across the creek, and follow the cascading stream to a small meadow with vistas of the surrounding peaks. Curve left on a horseshoe bend and return to the creek. Carefully wade across the creek again and head up canyon. At 3 miles, wade across to the west side of the creek. Follow the creek 0.6 miles to another horseshoe right bend. Begin the steep ascent of the mountain up numerous switchbacks for the next two miles. Near the top, the path breaks out onto the rocky plateau. Follow the cairns southwest to incredible views of the jagged rock walls of Sylvan Peak. Descend towards the cliffs across the rolling hills of the alpine plateau. This is our turnaround spot.

To hike further, the main trail continues southwest for 2 miles to Crow Lake. A faint trail descends to the left across the open tundra, reaching the Senia Creek Trail (Hike 17) at a prominent four-foot cairn above West Red Lodge Creek.

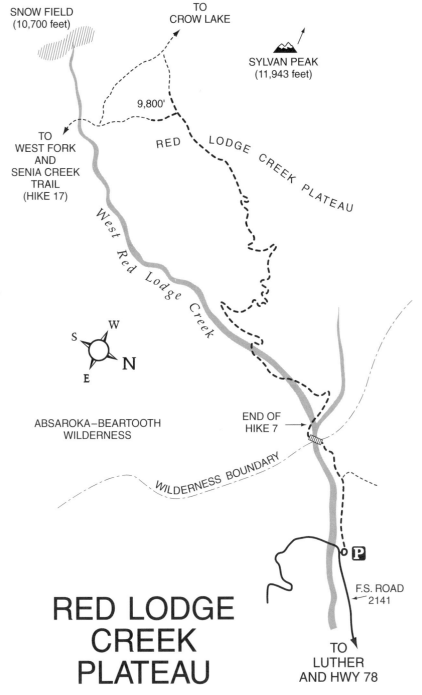

SNOW FIELD
(10,700 feet)

TO
CROW LAKE

SYLVAN PEAK
(11,943 feet)

9,800'

RED LODGE CREEK PLATEAU

TO
WEST FORK
AND
SENIA CREEK
TRAIL
(HIKE 17)

West Red Lodge Creek

S W
N
E

ABSAROKA–BEARTOOTH
WILDERNESS

END OF
HIKE 7

WILDERNESS BOUNDARY

P

F.S. ROAD
2141

TO
LUTHER
AND HWY 78

RED LODGE CREEK PLATEAU

Hike 9
Willow Creek Trail
from Palisades Campground

Hiking distance: 4 miles round trip
Hiking time: 2 hours
Elevation gain: 1,000 feet
Maps: R.M.S. Alpine-Mount Maurice
       U.S.G.S. Red Lodge West

Summary of hike: The Willow Creek Trail follows a lush forested canyon from Palisades Campground to Red Lodge Mountain ski area. The path closely winds along the contours of Willow Creek between limestone palisades and Grizzly Peak. The trail passes an old mining entrance and an old cabin. There are numerous creek crossings. At times the trail becomes faint.

Driving directions: From the south end of Red Lodge, turn right (west) on the road to Red Lodge Mountain ski area. At 1.1 mile, turn right at the signed turnoff to Palisades Campground. Drive 1.8 miles on the unpaved road to the far end of the campground. Park in the spaces on the right by the restrooms.

Hiking directions: Walk past the restrooms to the unsigned trailhead on the right by the log railing. Head up the forested path between Willow Creek and the limestone palisades. Cross a wooden footbridge over the creek. A short distance ahead is a trail fork. Detour for 20 yards to the right fork to a log crossing of Willow Creek by a deep rock cave. Return to the junction and take the main trail up the canyon, crossing over planks to the east side of the creek. At times the trail becomes faint for short distances. Closely follow the creek through the lush riparian terrain, and cross a talus slope as the canyon narrows. At 0.6 miles, cross the creek at a log jam, passing steep rock cliffs on the right. Watch for an old log cabin on the right, tucked into the hillside. Leave the drainage, and head up the wide path through a lodgepole pine forest to a trail split. Take the right fork to a log creek crossing at 1.1 mile. After crossing, continue upstream through the forest. Recross the stream to the left. Near the top of the draw cross to the east side of the creek, and walk through a sloping grass meadow. The trail ends at the head of the meadow by the ski area parking lot.

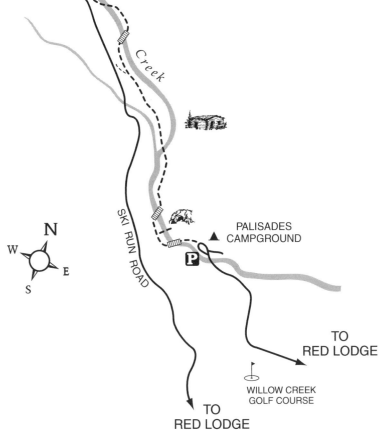

RED LODGE
MOUNTAIN

LIMESTONE PALISADES

GRIZZLY PEAK
(9,410 feet)

Willow

Creek

SKI RUN ROAD

PALISADES
CAMPGROUND

P

N
W   E
S

TO
RED LODGE

WILLOW CREEK
GOLF COURSE

TO
RED LODGE

WILLOW CREEK TRAIL

Hike 10
Nichols Creek Trail

Hiking distance: 4 miles round trip
Hiking time: 2 hours
Elevation gain: 1,100 feet
Maps: R.M.S. Alpine-Mount Maurice
      U.S.G.S. Red Lodge West

Summary of hike: The Nichols Creek Trail parallels Nichols Creek up a beautiful side drainage on the West Fork of Rock Creek by Red Lodge. The trail follows a rutted Forest Service road through aspen and pine groves to overlooks of the West Fork Canyon.

Driving directions: From the south end of Red Lodge, turn right (west) on the road to Red Lodge Mountain ski area. At 2.8 miles, turn left on West Fork Road. Continue 0.3 miles to Forest Service Road 2478, the first turnoff on the right. Turn right and park 40 yards ahead in the pullout on the right.

Hiking directions: Head north on the rough, unpaved road along the east side of Nichols Creek. The trail crosses open meadows with groves of aspens, pines and rock outcroppings. At 0.2 miles is a side road on the right. This detour follows the hillside 0.4 miles to an overlook of the West Fork Canyon, Rock Creek valley, Mount Maurice and the Pryor Mountains. Back on the main trail, rock hop across Nichols Creek to a trail split. The right fork leads 100 yards to a primitive campsite by the creek. The left fork heads up the east-facing hillside, entering a lodgepole pine forest. Continue uphill above Nichols Creek. At 1.4 miles, the trail curves left alongside the creek to a junction. The right fork parallels the creek for a quarter mile and ends in the lush grass and brush. The left fork climbs steeply up the mountain to a sharp right bend and overlook of the West Fork Canyon at 1.6 miles. This is a good turnaround spot.

To hike further, the trail steeply ascends the mountain through the dense forest to the 8,603-foot peak.

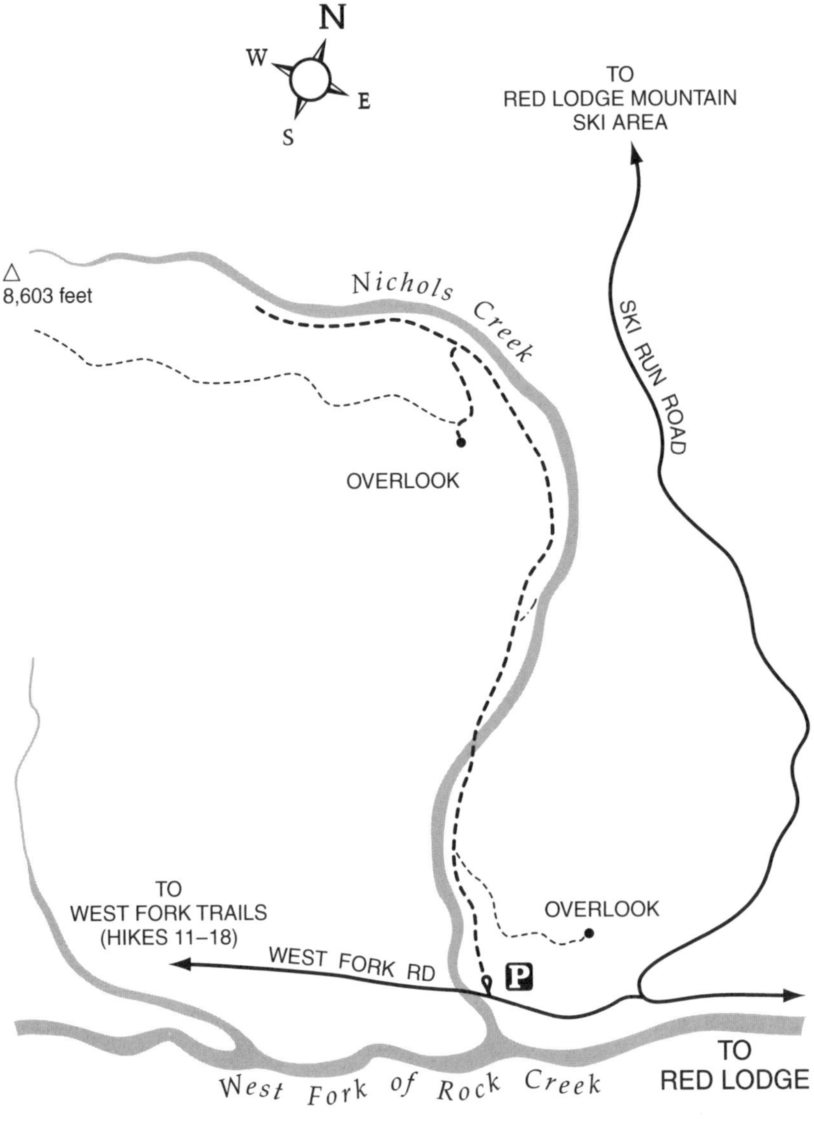

N
W E
S

TO
RED LODGE MOUNTAIN
SKI AREA

△
8,603 feet

Nichols Creek

SKI RUN ROAD

OVERLOOK

TO
WEST FORK TRAILS
(HIKES 11–18)

OVERLOOK

WEST FORK RD

P

West Fork of Rock Creek

TO
RED LODGE

NICHOLS CREEK
TRAIL

Hike 11
Silver Run Ski Trails

Hiking distance: 2.4—5 miles round trip
Hiking time: 1—2.5 hours
Elevation gain: 300 feet
Maps: R.M.S. Alpine-Mount Maurice
        U.S.G.S. Red Lodge West and Bare Mountain

Summary of hike: The Silver Run Ski Trails are popular trails for cross-country skiing. During the other half of the year, they are a great hiking and mountain biking get-away close to Red Lodge. The well-defined trails wind up the West Fork drainage along the canyon floor. The trails parallel the West Fork of Rock Creek and are surrounded by forested mountains.

Driving directions: From the south end of Red Lodge, turn right (west) on the road to Red Lodge Mountain ski area. At 2.8 miles, turn left on West Fork Road. Continue 1.6 miles to Silver Run Road and turn left. Drive 0.2 miles, crossing the creek, and park in the Silver Run Ski Trails parking area on the left.

Hiking directions: Hike west up the unpaved road, following the "Loop 1-4" sign to a road split. The left fork heads up Silver Run Creek. Take the right fork onto the trail. Fifty yards ahead is a second fork, which is the beginning of the loop. Bear left on the upper trail through the lodgepole pine forest. At 1.1 mile is a signed trail fork on the right to return on Loop 1, a 2.4-mile hike. Continue on the left to an old wooden hut and a rock stove. Just beyond the hut is a wooden bridge crossing Ingles Creek. After crossing, there is a signed junction with the Ingles Creek Trail (Hike 12). Bear right, staying on the Silver Run Trail to a junction at 2.1 miles. The right fork is the return for Loop 2, a 3-mile hike. For a longer hike, continue left on Loops 3 and 4. Loop 3 is a 4-mile hike and Loop 4 is a 5-mile hike. On Loop 4, cross a bridge over Basin Creek, and loop downhill towards the West Fork of Rock Creek. Parallel the West Fork downstream, returning to the trailhead.

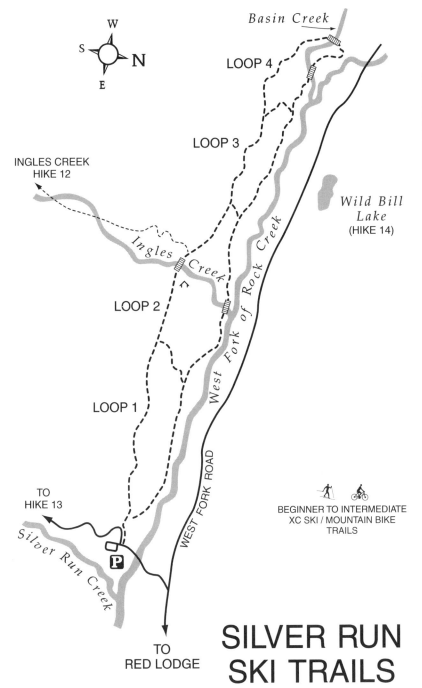

W N S E

Basin Creek

LOOP 4

LOOP 3

INGLES CREEK
HIKE 12

Ingles Creek

Wild Bill
Lake
(HIKE 14)

West Fork of Rock Creek

WEST FORK

LOOP 2

LOOP 1

TO
HIKE 13

Silver Run Creek

WEST FORK ROAD

P

BEGINNER TO INTERMEDIATE
XC SKI / MOUNTAIN BIKE
TRAILS

TO
RED LODGE

SILVER RUN
SKI TRAILS

Hike 12
Ingles Creek—Silver Run Plateau Loop

Hiking distance: 7 miles round trip
Hiking time: 3.5 hours
Elevation gain: 1,600 feet
Maps: R.M.S. Alpine-Mount Maurice
U.S.G.S. Red Lodge West, Mount Maurice, Bare Mtn.

Summary of hike: This loop hike begins on the Silver Run Ski Trail, parallel to the West Fork of Rock Creek. The trail ambles up a forested draw, crossing Ingles Creek seven times and passing three old logging cabins. The hike returns through the Silver Run drainage, following Silver Run Creek.

Driving directions: From the south end of Red Lodge, turn right (west) on the road to Red Lodge Mountain ski area. At 2.8 miles, turn left on West Fork Road. Continue 1.6 miles to Silver Run Road and turn left. Drive 0.2 miles, crossing the creek, and park in the Silver Run Ski Trails parking area on the left.

Hiking directions: Head west on the unpaved road to a road fork. Leave the road and begin the loop, bearing right on the signed Silver Run Ski Trail. Follow the blue trail signs 1.1 mile to a trail split. Stay left on Loop 2 to an old cabin and rock stove by Ingles Creek. Cross the wooden bridge over the creek to a signed junction. Bear left on the Ingles Creek Trail, and head up the Ingles Creek drainage on the serpentine path. A half mile up the canyon is the remains of an old miner's cabin. For the next two miles, the trail stays close to the creek and crosses it six times. A half mile after the sixth crossing are the remains of two more cabins on the left. Cross Ingles Creek to the left, and head up the west-facing hillside to a junction on the ridge of the Silver Run drainage (Hike 13). Bear left and zigzag down into the canyon. Cross a stream and continue downhill to Silver Run Creek. The trail ends at Forest Service Road 2476, the trailhead to Hike 13. Follow the unpaved road alongside Silver Run Creek for 1.9 miles, completing the loop. Return to the right.

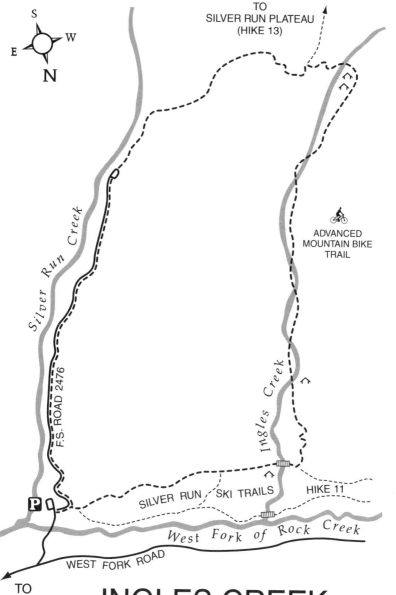

S
W
E
N

TO
SILVER RUN PLATEAU
(HIKE 13)

WEST FORK

Silver Run Creek

F.S. ROAD 2476

Ingles Creek

ADVANCED
MOUNTAIN BIKE
TRAIL

SILVER RUN   SKI TRAILS   HIKE 11

West Fork of Rock Creek

P

WEST FORK ROAD

TO
RED LODGE

INGLES CREEK–
SILVER RUN PLATEAU
LOOP

Hike 13
Silver Run Plateau Trail

Hiking distance: 8 miles round trip
Hiking time: 4 hours
Elevation gain: 2,400 feet
Maps: R.M.S. Alpine-Mount Maurice
U.S.G.S. Red Lodge West, Mount Maurice, Bare Mtn. and
Black Pyramid Mountain

Summary of hike: The Silver Run Plateau Trail climbs up the forested canyon to the wide open expanse of the Silver Run Plateau at over 10,000 feet. As you reach the plateau, the dense conifer forest gives way to dwarfed windswept trees and grassy alpine meadows. There are stunning panoramic views of the West Fork drainage down to Red Lodge, the eastern plains, the Lake Fork drainage to the Hellroaring Plateau, and Pyramid Mountain. (Be sure to bring warm clothing.)

Driving directions: From the south end of Red Lodge, turn right (west) on the road to Red Lodge Mountain ski area. At 2.8 miles, turn left on West Fork Road. Continue 1.6 miles to Silver Run Road and turn left. Drive 0.2 miles, crossing the creek to the Silver Run Ski Trails parking area on the left. Turn right on Forest Service Road 2476, and drive 1.9 miles to the signed trailhead parking area at the end of the road.

Hiking directions: Head west past the trailhead sign along the north side of Silver Run Creek. The trail, an old Forest Service stock road, soon veers away from the creek, winding up the canyon through an open forest. As the trail enters the dense forest, the trail steepens. At one mile is an unsigned trail split. (The left fork ends a half mile up the steep drainage.) Take the right fork and cross a small stream. At 1.2 miles, a switchback to the right leads to an overlook of the forested canyon. Continue uphill to an unsigned junction with the Ingles Creek Trail on the right (Hike 12). Stay left, following the mountain ridge between Silver Run and Ingles Creek drainages. From the ridge, the trail zigzags up through the forest to the Silver Run Plateau. Near the top, the forest gives way to stunted trees and grassy alpine meadows. The trail reaches the plateau at 3.5 miles. Cairns mark the trail across the plateau to a signed junction with the Beartrack Trail. This is our turnaround spot.

To hike further, the right fork heads to Timberline Lake (Hike 16), and the left fork descends to Highway 212 north of the Lake Fork of Rock Creek (Hike 21). These are popular shuttle hikes.

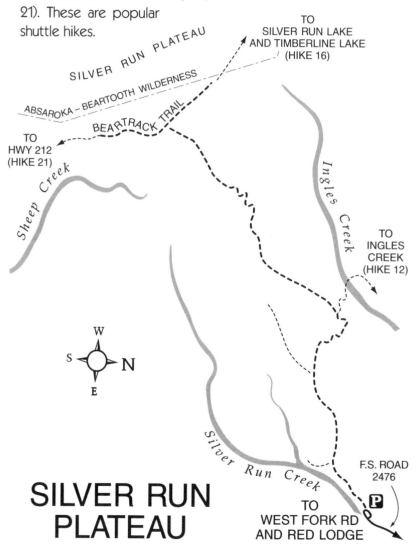

SILVER RUN PLATEAU

Hike 14
Wild Bill Lake

Hiking distance: 0.8 mile loop
Hiking time: 30 minutes
Elevation gain: Level hiking
Maps: R.M.S. Alpine-Mount Maurice
U.S.G.S. Red Lodge West

Summary of hike: Wild Bill Lake was created in a natural glacial depression by "Wild Bill" Kurtzer in 1902. Wild Bill stocked the lake and rented boats as a commercial venture. This trail circles the perimeter of the lake. There are two fishing docks extending out into the lake with sitting benches. One dock is located at the end of the peninsula. A picnic area with tables sits among the lodgepole pines on the east side of the lake by the parking lot. Wild Bill Lake is popular as a children's fishing area and is wheelchair accessible.

Driving directions: From the south end of Red Lodge, turn right (west) on the road to Red Lodge Mountain ski area. At 2.8 miles, turn left on West Fork Road. Continue 3.1 miles further to the Wild Bill Lake parking area on the right. Turn right and park.

Hiking directions: From the parking lot, walk north past the restrooms up to the bridge that crosses the lake spillway. The trail curves left to a Y-junction. The left fork leads to the peninsula. The right fork continues around the lake and back to the parking lot.

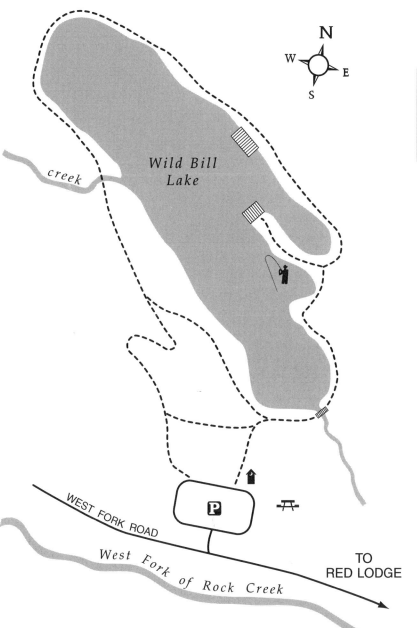

Wild Bill
Lake

creek

N

W

E

S

WEST FORK ROAD

West Fork of Rock Creek

P

TO
RED LODGE

WILD BILL LAKE

Hike 15
Basin Creek Lakes Trail

Hiking distance: 8 miles round trip
Hiking time: 4 hours
Elevation gain: 2,000 feet
Maps: R.M.S. Alpine-Mount Maurice
       U.S.G.S. Bare Mountain

Summary of hike: The trail to Lower and Upper Basin Creek Lakes is a gradual but steady uphill climb along a beautiful cascading stream. It passes a waterfall early on. The trail winds through evergreen forests and includes two log creek crossings. Lower Basin Creek Lake has an abundance of lily pads and is a very picturesque tarn. Upper Basin Creek Lake is at the base of a majestic mountain bowl just below the Silver Run Plateau. The snow melt empties into the lake.

Driving directions: From the south end of Red Lodge, turn right (west) on the road to Red Lodge Mountain ski area. At 2.8 miles, turn left on West Fork Road. Continue 4.2 miles further to the trailhead parking lot on the left. Turn left and park.

Hiking directions: From the parking lot, the wide trail heads uphill to the south along the whitewater of Basin Creek. The waterfall is 0.4 miles from the trailhead. As the trail curves to the right, climb some boulders along a spur trail to the left to view the two-tier waterfall. A short distance after the falls, the trail parallels Basin Creek to a log crossing over the creek. Continue uphill through the dense forest below the Silver Run Plateau, following the well-defined trail. The path passes several dilapidated log cabins, reaching Lower Basin Creek Lake at 2.7 miles. The steep trail continues past the lake through the thick pine forest, reaching Upper Basin Creek Lake at 3.8 miles.

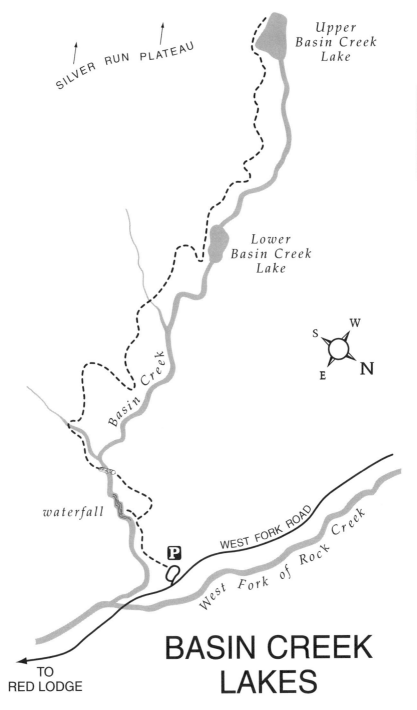

SILVER RUN PLATEAU

Upper Basin Creek Lake

Lower Basin Creek Lake

S W
E N

Basin Creek

waterfall

P

WEST FORK ROAD

West Fork of Rock Creek

TO
RED LODGE

BASIN CREEK
LAKES

Hike 16
Timberline and Gertrude Lakes

Hiking distance: 9 miles round trip
Hiking time: 4.5 hours
Elevation gain: 2,000 feet
Maps: R.M.S. Alpine-Mount Maurice
U.S.G.S. Bare Mountain & Sylvan Peak

Summary of hike: Timberline Lake sits in a basin below Silver Run Plateau at the base of a gorgeous granite cirque. Towering above the lake are snow-capped peaks, including the 12,500-foot Silver Run Peak. Lake Gertrude sits in a forested recess a half mile to the east. Both lakes lie within the Absaroka-Beartooth Wilderness and offer excellent trout fishing.

Driving directions: From the south end of Red Lodge, turn right (west) on the road to Red Lodge Mountain ski area. At 2.8 miles, turn left on West Fork Road. Continue 8.4 miles to the trailhead parking area on the left.

Hiking directions: From the parking area, hike southwest past the trailhead sign. The well-maintained trail is a gradual but steady uphill climb through an open forest. At one mile, the trail enters the Timberline Creek drainage where you can hear the creek tumbling down canyon. The trail crosses two tributaries and an unsigned junction with the Beartrack Trail at three miles. Take the fork to the right along the west side of Timberline Creek. The trail winds past a mosaic of trickling streams and memorable views of the surrounding peaks. At 3.8 miles is a log crossing over Timberline Creek. After crossing, the trail enters the Absaroka-Beartooth Wilderness and approaches the east end of Gertrude Lake. Continue along the south side of the lake, crossing logs over two inlet streams. Continue upstream less than a half mile to an outlet pond and Timberline Lake at the trail's end. Fisherman trails lead around this lake that sits in a broad cirque.

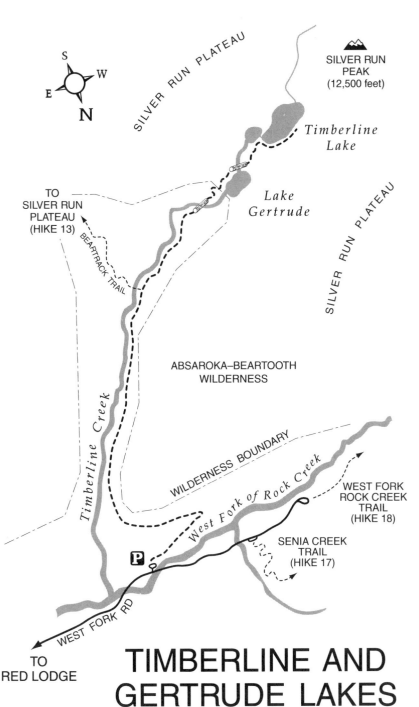

SILVER RUN PLATEAU

SILVER RUN
PEAK
(12,500 feet)

S W
E
N

Timberline Lake

TO
SILVER RUN
PLATEAU
(HIKE 13)

Lake Gertrude

BEARTRACK TRAIL

SILVER RUN PLATEAU

ABSAROKA–BEARTOOTH
WILDERNESS

Timberline Creek

WILDERNESS BOUNDARY

West Fork of Rock Creek

WEST FORK
ROCK CREEK
TRAIL
(HIKE 18)

SENIA CREEK
TRAIL
(HIKE 17)

P

WEST FORK RD

TO
RED LODGE

TIMBERLINE AND
GERTRUDE LAKES

Hike 17
Senia Creek Trail to Red Lodge Creek Plateau

Hiking distance: 8.2 miles round trip (or 12-mile shuttle)
Hiking time: 4 hours
Elevation gain: 2,600 feet
Maps: R.M.S. Alpine-Mount Maurice
　　　 U.S.G.S. Bare Mountain and Sylvan Peak

Summary of hike: The Senia Creek Trail climbs from the West Fork Canyon to the Red Lodge Creek Plateau. The trail crosses the plateau and connects with trails to Crow Lake, Sylvan Lake, East Rosebud Lake and down the West Red Lodge Creek Trail to the town of Luther. This hike switchbacks up the forested southern flank of Bare Mountain, then crosses the alpine plateau and descends 400 feet to the tree-lined West Red Lodge Creek. The vistas from this high altitude plateau are stunning. This hike may be combined with the West Red Lodge Creek Trail (Hike 8) for a 12-mile shuttle hike. (Bring warm clothing.)

Driving directions: From the south end of Red Lodge, turn right (west) on the road to Red Lodge Mountain ski area. At 2.8 miles, turn left on the West Fork Road. Continue 9 miles to the signed trailhead parking area on the right side of the road.

Hiking directions: Head up the signed trail, soon entering the Absaroka-Beartooth Wilderness. Switchbacks lead up through the forest to the Senia Creek drainage at 1.6 miles. The trail levels out at 2.5 miles as the forest thins near the plateau. Views open up in all directions, from the eastern plains to the Silver Run Plateau. Once on the Red Lodge Creek Plateau, the gravel trail is marked with cairns. Cross the plateau, reaching 9,980 feet—the highest point on the trail—at 3.9 miles. Descend 400 feet to the West Red Lodge Creek drainage. The tree-lined, cascading creek is a good spot to take a break and marvel at the views. Return along the same path.

To hike further, rock hop across the creek and take the path to the right, heading up the hill. Around the bend on the ridge is a four-foot cairn. The clearly defined trail to the left leads to Crow Lake 2 miles ahead. The faint right fork crosses the open expanse and several meandering streams, connecting with the West Red Lodge Creek Trail at the ridge (Hike 8).

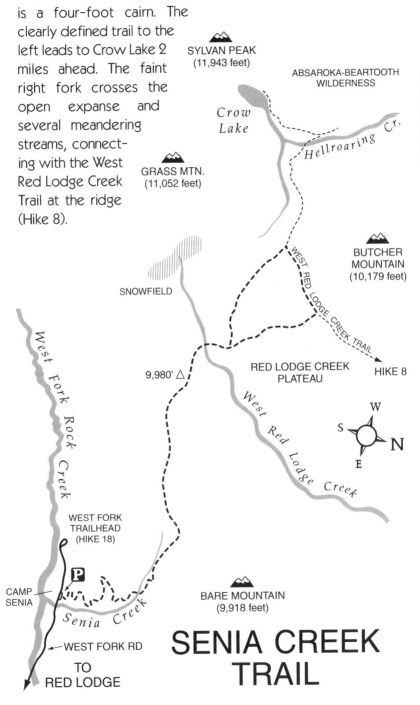

SYLVAN PEAK
(11,943 feet)

ABSAROKA-BEARTOOTH
WILDERNESS

Crow Lake

Hellroaring Cr.

GRASS MTN.
(11,052 feet)

BUTCHER MOUNTAIN
(10,179 feet)

WEST RED LODGE CREEK TRAIL

SNOWFIELD

9,980' △

RED LODGE CREEK PLATEAU

HIKE 8

West Red Lodge Creek

West Fork Rock Creek

WEST FORK TRAILHEAD
(HIKE 18)

P

CAMP SENIA

Senia Creek

BARE MOUNTAIN
(9,918 feet)

WEST FORK RD

TO RED LODGE

SENIA CREEK TRAIL

Hike 18
West Fork of Rock Creek

Hiking distance and time:

        3 miles round trip to Calamity Falls: 1.5 hours

        5 miles round trip to Sentinel Falls: 2.5 hours

        8 miles round trip to Quinnebaugh Meadows: 4 hours

        10 miles round trip to Lake Mary: 5 hours

Elevation gain: 350 feet

Maps: R.M.S. Alpine-Mount Maurice

      U.S.G.S. Sylvan Peak, Bare Mountain

Summary of hike: The roaring sounds of the West Fork are always nearby on this hike. Various trickling brooks flow close to the path. The trail winds through the forest and open boulder fields that overlook Rock Creek and the sculptured peaks of Elk and Bowback Mountains. It passes two magnificent waterfalls cutting through rock canyon walls. Both are good lunch spots, with flat rocks for seating. This trail is part of the 19-mile hike that crosses Sundance Pass and ends at the Lake Fork of Rock Creek (Hike 23), a popular shuttle hike.

Driving directions: From the south end of Red Lodge, turn right (west) onto the road to Red Lodge Mountain ski area. At 2.8 miles, turn left on West Fork Road. Continue 10 miles to the trailhead at the end of the road and park.

Hiking directions: Take the trail on the north side of the parking area. It is well maintained and easy to follow. The trail passes several boulder fields en route to Calamity Falls, about 1.5 miles. The waterfall is not visible from the trail. Listen for the sound of the falls and watch for a side trail on the left that leads to the falls. Sentinel Falls is one mile further along the main trail. This falls is easy to spot and enjoy from the trail. Above Sentinel Falls, the creek opens up to a beautiful, wide body of water. Quinnebaugh Meadows is one mile further. From the meadow, you may take a side trip to Lake Mary, a steep, uphill one-mile hike. To return, retrace your steps.

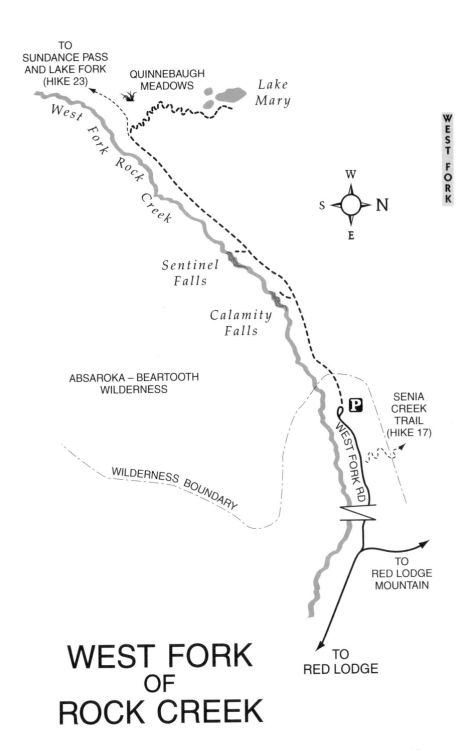

TO
SUNDANCE PASS
AND LAKE FORK
(HIKE 23)

QUINNEBAUGH
MEADOWS

*Lake
Mary*

West Fork Rock Creek

W

S   N

E

*Sentinel
Falls*

*Calamity
Falls*

ABSAROKA – BEARTOOTH
WILDERNESS

P

SENIA
CREEK
TRAIL
(HIKE 17)

WEST FORK RD

WILDERNESS BOUNDARY

TO
RED LODGE
MOUNTAIN

TO
RED LODGE

WEST FORK
OF
ROCK CREEK

Hike 19
Maurice Creek Trail
to Line Creek Plateau

Hiking distance: 9 miles round trip
Hiking time: 4.5 hours
Elevation gain: 3,200 feet
Maps: R.M.S. Alpine-Mount Maurice
      U.S.G.S. Mount Maurice

Summary of hike: The Maurice Creek Trail heads up Mount Maurice to the Line Creek Plateau. The trail stays high above Maurice Creek through a pine forest. It is a strenuous 3,200-foot hike up a beautiful stream-fed canyon.

Driving directions: From downtown Red Lodge, drive 5 miles south on Highway 212 to the signed East Side Road turnoff on the left, between mile markers 64 and 65. Turn left and continue 0.5 miles, crossing Rock Creek, to the signed Maurice Creek Trail on the left. Turn left and park.

Hiking directions: Walk up the road and pass through a cattle gate. Head gently uphill to Maurice Creek, the only time that the trail meets the creek. Curve right up the hillside overlooking Rock Creek Resort and the canyon. Switchbacks lead uphill, entering a conifer forest in the Maurice Creek drainage. At 2 miles, the trail reaches a ridge and temporarily levels out. Cross the trickling tributary stream of Seeley Creek at 7,800 feet. This is a turnaround spot for a short hike. It is the mid-point of the hike in miles and elevation. A short distance ahead, a series of eight switchbacks skirt past the west side of the peak. The trail finally reaches the northeast edge of the exposed plateau at 4.5 miles. This is a good turnaround spot.

To hike further, follow the faint path through the alpine corridor to the wide expanse of the Line Creek Plateau at 6 miles. Widespread cairns mark the path across the plateau. The trail connects with the Corral Creek Trail (Hike 20) at 9 miles and continues to the Highline Trail Lakes (Hike 28) at the state line.

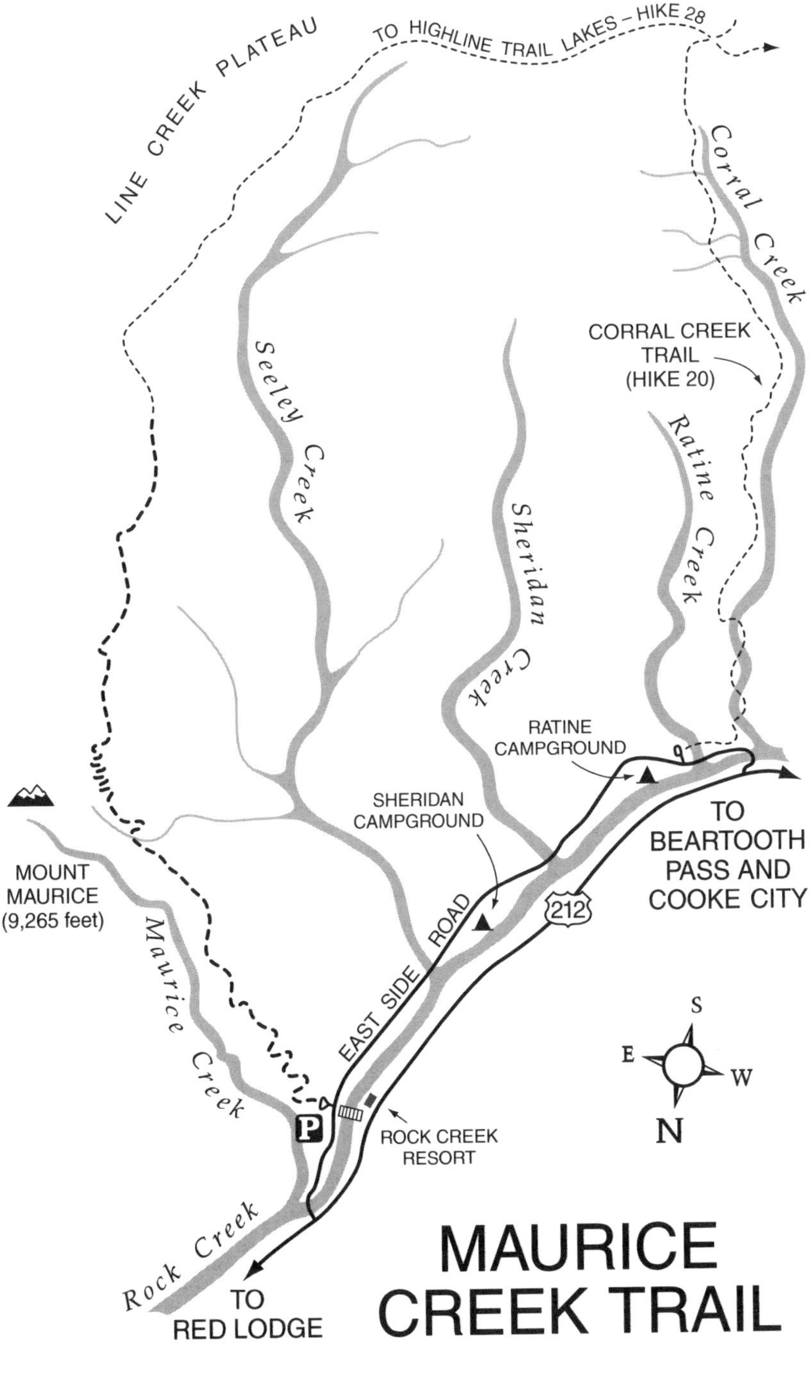

LINE CREEK PLATEAU

TO HIGHLINE TRAIL LAKES – HIKE 28

Corral Creek

CORRAL CREEK
TRAIL
(HIKE 20)

MAIN FORK

Seeley Creek

Sheridan Creek

Ratine Creek

RATINE
CAMPGROUND

SHERIDAN
CAMPGROUND

TO
BEARTOOTH
PASS AND
COOKE CITY

MOUNT
MAURICE
(9,265 feet)

212

EAST SIDE ROAD

Maurice Creek

P

ROCK CREEK
RESORT

S
E ⊕ W
N

Rock Creek

TO
RED LODGE

MAURICE
CREEK TRAIL

Hike 20
Corral Creek Trail to Line Creek Plateau

Hiking distance: 8 miles round trip
Hiking time: 4 hours
Elevation gain: 3,200 feet
Maps: R.M.S. Alpine-Mount Maurice
U.S.G.S. Mount Maurice

Summary of hike: The Corral Creek Trail follows a narrow mountain drainage curving around Sheridan Point. The trail leads to the headwaters of Corral Creek on the Line Creek Plateau. The well-defined trail has five creek crossings in the first mile. It is a beautiful but strenuous hike, gaining more than 3,000 feet.

Driving directions: From downtown Red Lodge, drive 8 miles south on Highway 212 to the second signed East Side Road turnoff on the left, between mile markers 61 and 62. Turn left and continue 0.3 miles, crossing Rock Creek, to the Corral Creek trailhead parking area on the right. It is across from the Ratine Campground.

Hiking directions: Hike past the trailhead sign and cross Ratine Creek. Follow the trail signs past the summer cabins, and head up the canyon between Ratine Creek and Corral Creek. At 0.3 miles, cross over Corral Creek two times by large mossy boulders. Parallel the banks of the creek up the west-facing hill. Cross a log bridge over the creek, and continue past cascades and pools, heading up the narrow canyon. At 0.8 miles, cross to the east side of the creek, and head up the hillside, leaving the creek. Head steadily up the canyon while curving around the west flank of Sheridan Point. Cross three trickling streams to the head of the canyon. Break out of the forest onto the picturesque meadowlands on the Line Creek Plateau by the Corral Creek headwaters. Cross the trailless rolling slopes along the rocky drainage to a five-foot rock cairn. Heading right, across the plateau, leads to the Highline Trail Lakes (Hike 28) at the state line. To the left is the Maurice Creek Trail (Hike 19).

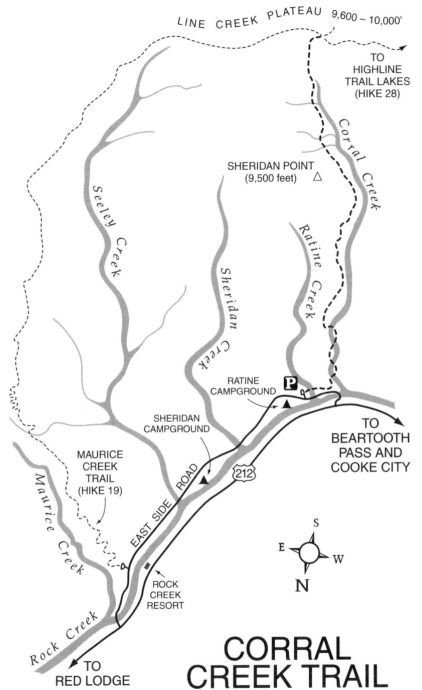

LINE CREEK PLATEAU 9,600 – 10,000'

TO
HIGHLINE
TRAIL LAKES
(HIKE 28)

Corral Creek

SHERIDAN POINT
(9,500 feet) △

Seeley Creek

Sheridan Creek

Ratine Creek

RATINE
CAMPGROUND

P

SHERIDAN
CAMPGROUND

TO
BEARTOOTH
PASS AND
COOKE CITY

MAURICE
CREEK
TRAIL
(HIKE 19)

EAST SIDE ROAD

212

Maurice Creek

ROCK
CREEK
RESORT

S
E   W
N

Rock Creek

TO
RED LODGE

CORRAL
CREEK TRAIL

Fifty-eight Great Hikes - **49**

Hike 21
Beartrack Trail to Silver Run Plateau

Hiking distance: 8 miles round trip
Hiking time: 4 hours
Elevation gain: 2,900 feet
Maps: R.M.S. Alpine-Mount Maurice
       U.S.G.S. Mount Maurice and Black Pyramid Mountain

Summary of hike: The Beartrack Trail climbs from Rock Creek Canyon to the Silver Run Plateau at 10,000 feet. Along the way are great views up and down the canyon, including the surrounding peaks of Mount Maurice, Tolman Mountain and Black Pyramid Mountain. The trail begins just west of the burn area from the 2000 fire. The trail then crosses the windswept alpine plateau and connects with the Silver Run Plateau Trail (Hike 13). You may combine this trail with Hike 13 for an 8-mile shuttle hike. Be sure to bring warm clothing.

Driving directions: From downtown Red Lodge, drive 9.5 miles south on Highway 212 to the turnoff on the right between mile markers 59 and 60. Turn right and park 20 yards ahead by the trailhead sign.

Hiking directions: Cross the meadows towards Wapiti Mountain, then curve left, traversing the foothills towards Tolman Point. Cross a stream, then a footbridge over Sheep Creek, entering the evergreen forest. Continue west to a signed junction. The left fork leads 40 yards to a log crossing at Snow Creek. Take the right fork and begin the ascent, crossing talus slopes and aspen groves. Switchbacks lead steadily uphill, but it is rarely steep. The trail levels out near an 8,800-foot knoll. Head uphill again, breaking out of the trees to the Silver Run Plateau at over 10,000 feet. Follow the cairns across the alpine tundra to a signed junction. The Silver Run Plateau Trail descends into the West Fork of Rock Creek (Hike 13). The left fork continues straight ahead, also descending to the West Fork at the Timberline Lake trailhead (Hike 16).

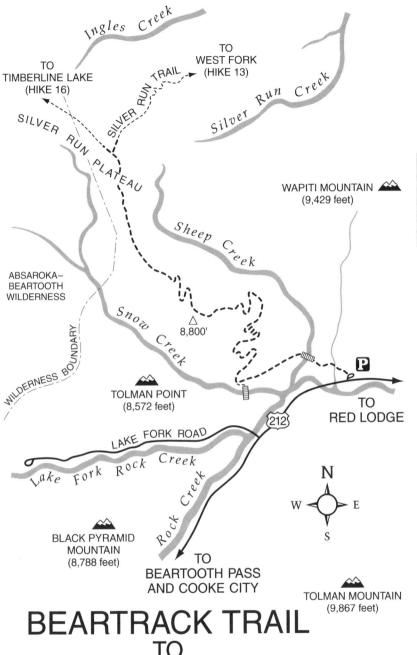

Ingles Creek

TO
TIMBERLINE LAKE
(HIKE 16)

SILVER RUN TRAIL

TO
WEST FORK
(HIKE 13)

Silver Run Creek

SILVER RUN PLATEAU

MAIN FORK

WAPITI MOUNTAIN
(9,429 feet)

Sheep Creek

ABSAROKA–
BEARTOOTH
WILDERNESS

Snow Creek

△
8,800'

WILDERNESS BOUNDARY

P

TO
RED LODGE

TOLMAN POINT
(8,572 feet)

212

LAKE FORK ROAD

Lake Fork Rock Creek

Rock Creek

N

W   E

S

BLACK PYRAMID
MOUNTAIN
(8,788 feet)

TO
BEARTOOTH PASS
AND COOKE CITY

TOLMAN MOUNTAIN
(9,867 feet)

BEARTRACK TRAIL
TO
SILVER RUN PLATEAU

Hike 22
Lower Lake Fork Trail

Hiking distance: 2.9 miles round trip
Hiking time: 1.5 hours
Elevation gain: 350 feet
Maps: R.M.S. Alpine-Mount Maurice
 U.S.G.S. Black Pyramid Mountain

Summary of hike: The Lower Lake Fork Trail follows the raging whitewater of the Lake Fork through a forest of lodgepole pine and aspen. The well-defined path heads west along the north flank of Black Pyramid Mountain past cascades, pools and small waterfalls. Moose are often spotted in the area. The Lake Fork Canyon is a popular cross-country ski trail in winter.

Driving directions: From Red Lodge, drive 10 miles south on Highway 212 to mile marker 59. Turn right at the Lake Fork Road—a sign marks the turn. Drive 0.8 miles to a paved parking pullout on the left.

Hiking directions: Descend from either end of the parking area, and take the footpath 20 yards to the left. Cross the wooden bridge over the Lake Fork, and head upstream to the right. The forested path, carpeted with pine needles, follows the watercourse of the cascading Lake Fork. At 1.2 miles, the trail reaches a wooden bridge that crosses the creek to the Lake Fork Trail parking lot. The main trail continues straight ahead to Lost Lake (Hike 23). Return by retracing your steps back to the lower bridge.

To hike further, continue following the creek downstream. At a quarter mile, the trail breaks out of the forest into a meadow with views of Tolman Mountain across Rock Creek Canyon. The trail enters the Billings Lion Youth Camp from the meadow. This is our turnaround spot. Return the way you came.

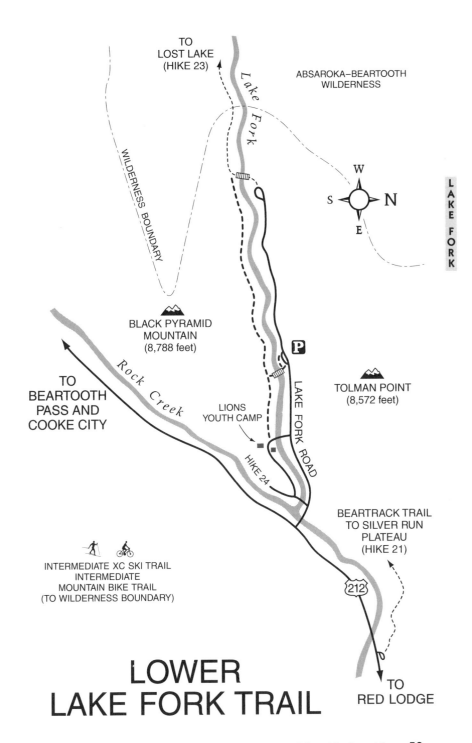

TO
LOST LAKE
(HIKE 23)

ABSAROKA–BEARTOOTH
WILDERNESS

Lake Fork

WILDERNESS BOUNDARY

LAKE FORK

BLACK PYRAMID
MOUNTAIN
(8,788 feet)

Rock Creek

TO
BEARTOOTH
PASS AND
COOKE CITY

P

TOLMAN POINT
(8,572 feet)

LIONS
YOUTH CAMP

LAKE FORK ROAD

HIKE 24

BEARTRACK TRAIL
TO SILVER RUN
PLATEAU
(HIKE 21)

INTERMEDIATE XC SKI TRAIL
INTERMEDIATE
MOUNTAIN BIKE TRAIL
(TO WILDERNESS BOUNDARY)

212

LOWER
LAKE FORK TRAIL

TO
RED LODGE

Hike 23
Lake Fork Trail

Hiking distance: 10 miles round trip
Hiking time: 5 hours
Elevation gain: 600 feet
Maps: R.M.S. Alpine-Mount Maurice
      U.S.G.S. Black Pyramid Mountain, Silver Run Peak

Summary of hike: Located south of Red Lodge in Lake Fork Canyon, the Lake Fork Trail follows a beautiful mountain creek through a lodgepole pine forest to a series of lakes. This popular trail follows the south edge of the Lake Fork of Rock Creek all the way up the canyon. Silver Falls, a long, thin waterfall, can be seen flowing down the mountain on the far left. Lake Fork Canyon is a popular cross-country ski area in the winter. This trail may be combined with the West Fork Rock Creek Trail (Hike 18) for a 19-mile shuttle hike that crosses Sundance Pass.

Driving directions: From Red Lodge, drive 10 miles south on Highway 212 to mile marker 59. Turn right at the Lake Fork Road—a sign marks the turn. Drive 2 miles to the end of the road. Park in the trailhead parking lot.

Hiking directions: The trailhead begins at the end of the parking lot. Cross the bridge over Lake Fork and turn right, heading up canyon. Continue along the well-defined trail parallel to the creek. At 0.3 miles, the trail enters the Absaroka-Beartooth Wilderness. At one mile, there is a rocky creekside beach. To the left, Silver Falls can be seen on the north-facing cliffs. The first lake is Broadwater Lake at 3.5 miles. Lost Lake is 5 miles up, making a 10-mile round trip. This area is so beautiful that if you choose not to hike all the way up to Lost Lake, the hike will still be a wonderful experience. At Lost Lake is a signed junction. The right fork heads uphill to Keyser Brown Lake (2 more miles) and September Morn Lake. This trail is part of a 19-mile hike that crosses Sundance Pass and ends at the West Fork of Rock Creek (Hike 18).

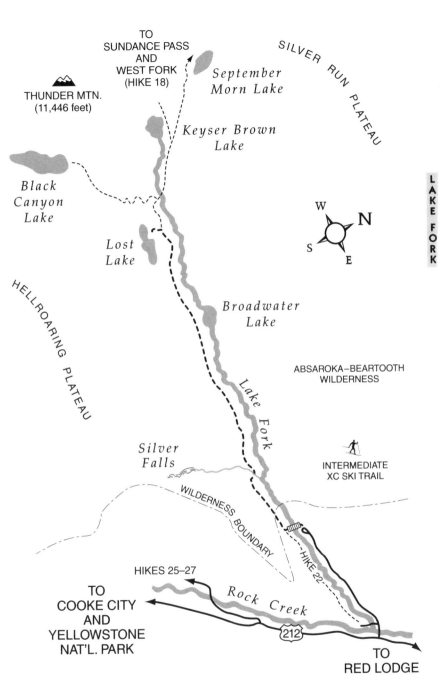

TO
SUNDANCE PASS
AND
WEST FORK
(HIKE 18)

September Morn Lake

SILVER RUN PLATEAU

THUNDER MTN.
(11,446 feet)

Keyser Brown Lake

Black Canyon Lake

W
N
S
E

Lost Lake

Broadwater Lake

ABSAROKA–BEARTOOTH
WILDERNESS

HELLROARING PLATEAU

Lake Fork

Silver Falls

INTERMEDIATE
XC SKI TRAIL

WILDERNESS BOUNDARY

HIKE 22

HIKES 25–27

Rock Creek

TO
COOKE CITY
AND
YELLOWSTONE
NAT'L. PARK

212

TO
RED LODGE

LAKE
FORK

LAKE FORK TRAIL

Hike 24
Rock Creek Streamside Trail

Hiking distance: 4.4 miles round trip
Hiking time: 2 hours
Elevation gain: 400 feet
Maps: R.M.S. Alpine-Mount Maurice
       U.S.G.S. Black Pyramid Mountain

Summary of hike: The Rock Creek Streamside Trail gently follows an unpaved forested road along the cascading white-water of Rock Creek. The road, closed to vehicles, begins at the Lake Fork in Rock Creek Canyon and parallels the creek upstream along the base of Black Pyramid Mountain. The trail ends on the Hellroaring Plateau Road at the Greenough and Limber Pine Campgrounds.

Driving directions: From Red Lodge, drive 10 miles south on Highway 212 to mile marker 59. Turn right at the Lake Fork Road—a sign marks the turn. Drive over the Rock Creek bridge and turn left. Immediately cross the bridge over Lake Fork, and continue 0.2 miles to boulders crossing the road. Park along the side of the road.

Hiking directions: Head southwest up the old road past the boulders. Enter the pine and aspen forest above the thunderous cascades of Rock Creek. Follow the forested path along the east flank of Black Pyramid Mountain. Various side paths lead down to the edge of Rock Creek. At one mile, the trail climbs up a small hill and out of the forest, giving way to the open area dotted with evergreens. Views of the surrounding mountains stretch up and down the glacier-scoured canyon. The trail veers away from Rock Creek to the unpaved Hellroaring Plateau Road at 2.2 miles. To the right, the road leads up to the plateau (Hike 26). To the left, the road leads to the Greenough Campground and the Greenough Lake Trailhead (Hike 25). Return to the trailhead the way you came.

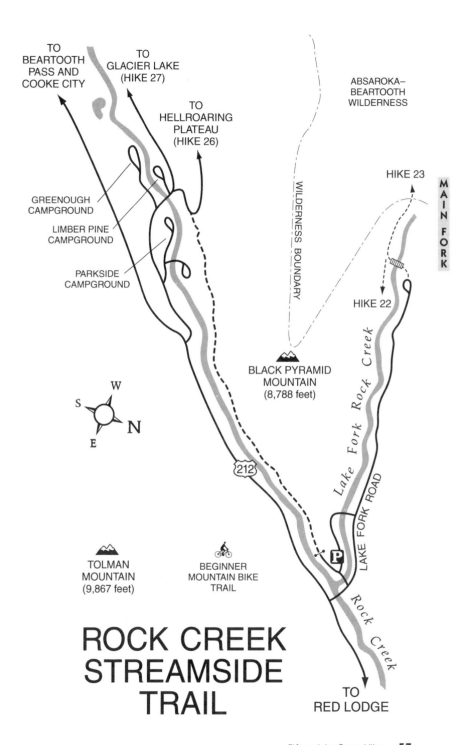

TO
BEARTOOTH
PASS AND
COOKE CITY

TO
GLACIER LAKE
(HIKE 27)

TO
HELLROARING
PLATEAU
(HIKE 26)

ABSAROKA–
BEARTOOTH
WILDERNESS

HIKE 23

MAIN FORK

GREENOUGH
CAMPGROUND

LIMBER PINE
CAMPGROUND

PARKSIDE
CAMPGROUND

WILDERNESS BOUNDARY

HIKE 22

W

S   N

E

Lake Fork Rock Creek

BLACK PYRAMID
MOUNTAIN
(8,788 feet)

212

LAKE FORK ROAD

TOLMAN
MOUNTAIN
(9,867 feet)

BEGINNER
MOUNTAIN BIKE
TRAIL

P

Rock Creek

ROCK CREEK
STREAMSIDE
TRAIL

TO
RED LODGE

Hike 25
Parkside National Recreation Trail from Greenough Trailhead

Hiking distance: 3 miles round trip
Hiking time: 1.5 hours
Elevation gain: 200 feet
Maps: R.M.S. Alpine-Mount Maurice
U.S.G.S. Black Pyramid Mountain

Summary of hike: The Parkside National Recreation Trail leads to Greenough Lake, a tree-lined, one-acre lake in Rock Creek Canyon. The lake is a popular fishing hole stocked with rainbow trout. Beyond Greenough Lake, the trail passes through pine forests and open meadows between the Hellroaring Plateau and the switchbacks up to the Beartooth Plateau.

Driving directions: From Red Lodge, take Highway 212 south 11.5 miles to the signed Rock Creek Road turnoff on the right. Turn right and drive 0.8 miles to the Greenough Lake Trail and campground on the left, just after crossing Wyoming Creek. Turn left and go 0.3 miles to the trailhead parking lot at the south end of the campground.

Hiking directions: Walk south past the trailhead sign through a lodgepole pine forest to an unsigned trail split. The left fork follows the old road, and the right fork is a footpath along the banks of Rock Creek. At a quarter mile both trails rejoin at Greenough Lake. Curve right, looping around the west side of the lake. At one mile, the trail breaks out of the trees into a large meadow. To the west are the switchbacks up to the Hellroaring Plateau. To the east are the switchbacks up to the Beartooth Plateau. Walk through the meadow and reenter the forest. At 1.5 miles, cross the wooden footbridge over cascading Quad Creek to the M-K Trailhead near the M-K Campground. This is our turnaround spot. Return along the same path or follow the gravel road back to the Greenough Lake Campground for a loop hike.

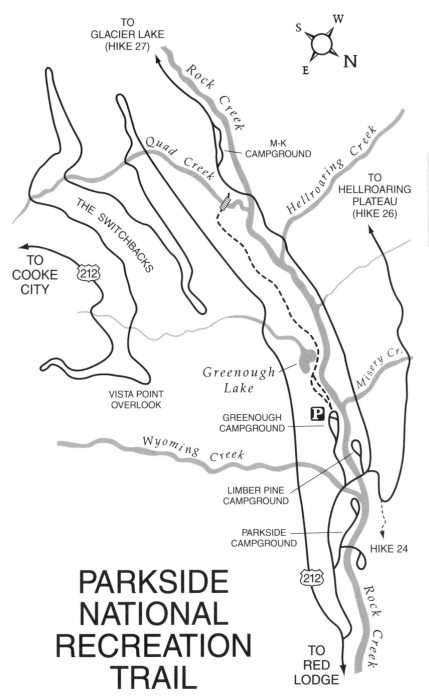

TO
GLACIER LAKE
(HIKE 27)

Rock Creek

S W
N
E

Quad Creek

M-K
CAMPGROUND

Hellroaring Creek

TO
HELLROARING
PLATEAU
(HIKE 26)

THE SWITCHBACKS

212

TO
COOKE
CITY

Misery Cr.

Greenough Lake

VISTA POINT
OVERLOOK

P

GREENOUGH
CAMPGROUND

Wyoming Creek

LIMBER PINE
CAMPGROUND

PARKSIDE
CAMPGROUND

HIKE 24

Rock Creek

212

PARKSIDE NATIONAL RECREATION TRAIL

TO
RED
LODGE

MAIN FORK

Hike 26
Hellroaring Plateau

Hiking distance: 6 miles round trip
Hiking time: 3 hours to all day
Elevation gain: 600 feet
Maps: R.M.S. Alpine-Mount Maurice
U.S.G.S. Black Pyramid and Silver Run Peak

Summary of hike: The Hellroaring Plateau is a vast, top-of-the-world alpine tundra lying above 10,000 feet. Although the elevation gain of this hike is gradual, at this height the gain feels more substantial. From the trailhead, there are great views up Rock Creek Canyon and the Beartooth Highway switchbacks across the valley. This hike accesses a beautiful alpine basin filled with a chain of 14 lakes. Many of the lakes offer excellent fishing. Be prepared with warm and protective clothing, as the weather changes abruptly. It is wise to have a topographic map.

Driving directions: From Red Lodge, take Highway 212 south 11.5 miles to the signed Rock Creek Road turnoff on the right. Turn right and continue 0.9 miles to the Glacier Lake/Hellroaring Plateau road split. Take the right fork towards the Hellroaring Plateau, and continue up a grueling 5.8 miles to the trailhead parking area at road's end. The last 5 miles of the road are steep, rough, winding and narrow.

Hiking directions: From the parking area, the trail heads west past the trailhead sign. The trail—an old jeep road—gains elevation gradually along the vast alpine plateau. At one mile, views into the valley basin open to four lower Hellroaring Lakes. Stay on the plateau, continuing to the west as the trail veers left and back to the right. A side trail heads off to the left, leading to an overlook of the Rock Creek drainage. At 1.6 miles, just before reaching an enormous snowfield, a trail on the right leads down to the Hellroaring Lakes. Down at the lakes, fishermen trails lead to every lake. After fishing or exploring, hike back to the plateau and return along the same route.

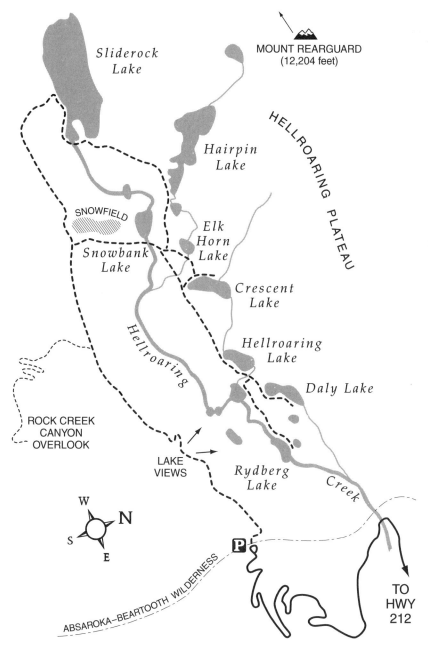

MOUNT REARGUARD
(12,204 feet)

Sliderock
Lake

HELLROARING PLATEAU

Hairpin
Lake

SNOWFIELD

Elk
Horn
Lake

Snowbank
Lake

Crescent
Lake

Hellroaring
Lake

Hellroaring

Daly Lake

ROCK CREEK
CANYON
OVERLOOK

LAKE
VIEWS

Rydberg
Lake

Creek

W
N
S
E

P

ABSAROKA–BEARTOOTH WILDERNESS

TO
HWY
212

HELLROARING PLATEAU

Hike 27
Glacier Lake

distance: 4 miles round trip
Hiking time: 2.5 hours
Elevation gain: 1,000 feet
Maps: R.M.S. Alpine-Mount Maurice
U.S.G.S. Silver Run Peak

Summary of hike: Glacier Lake, at 9,700 feet, sits in a bowl surrounded by mountains at the head of Rock Creek Canyon. It is the largest lake in the Rock Creek drainage and is the headwaters of Rock Creek. The steady climb up to Glacier Lake follows the swift, cascading Moon Creek for a half mile, then crosses the creek on a log bridge. There are stunning views of the glacier-carved canyon and fascinating twisted old trees.

Driving directions: From Red Lodge, take Highway 212 south 11.5 miles to the signed Rock Creek Road turnoff on the right. Turn right and drive 0.9 miles, crossing Wyoming Creek, to a road fork at the end of the paved road. Bear left and drive 7 miles on the unpaved road to the parking lot at the end of the road. The road becomes rocky as you near the trailhead.

Hiking directions: Head northwest past the signed trailhead, steadily climbing up the mountainside. Switchbacks zigzag up the slope to minimize the steep grade. Cross a bridge over Moon Creek at 0.5 miles. After crossing, a narrow, unsigned side path bears to the right, heading north up to Shelf Lake and Moon Lake at the base of Mount Rearguard. Bear left (west), staying on the main trail to a ridge above Glacier Lake. From the ridge is a great view of the massive lake and the surrounding mountains. Descend to the northeastern shoreline by the dam. An angler trail bears right along the northeast side of the lake. After exploring the area, return along the same trail.

For an interesting side trip, take the faint trail up Moon Creek for a half mile to some huge boulders which have tumbled into the drainage.

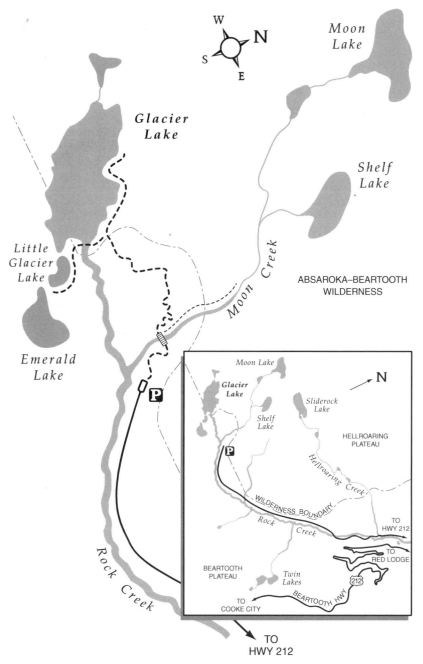

W
N
S
E

Moon Lake

Glacier Lake

Shelf Lake

Little Glacier Lake

ABSAROKA–BEARTOOTH
WILDERNESS

Moon Creek

Emerald Lake

P

Rock Creek

N

Moon Lake

Glacier Lake

Shelf Lake

Sliderock Lake

HELLROARING
PLATEAU

P

Hellroaring Creek

WILDERNESS BOUNDARY

Rock Creek

TO
HWY 212

TO
RED LODGE

BEARTOOTH
PLATEAU

Twin Lakes

212

TO
COOKE CITY

BEARTOOTH HWY

TO
HWY 212

GLACIER LAKE

Hike 28
Highline Trail Lakes
on Line Creek Plateau

Hiking distance: 4 miles round trip
Hiking time: 2 hours
Elevation gain: 300 feet
Maps: R.M.S. Alpine-Mount Maurice and Wyoming Beartooths
U.S.G.S. Black Pyramid Mountain and Deep Lake

Summary of hike: The Highline Trail Lakes are a series of ten lakes in an ice-scoured depression on the exposed 10,000-foot alpine plateau. The lakes rest at the south end of Line Creek Plateau near the headwaters of Wyoming Creek. The Highline Creek Trail straddles the Montana-Wyoming state line.

Driving directions: The trailhead is located on Highway 212—24 miles from Red Lodge and 40.3 miles from Cooke City. The trailhead turnoff is a half mile north of the Montana-Wyoming state line. Turn south and drive 0.2 miles to the parking area at the end of the road.

Hiking directions: Head downhill across the exposed alpine tundra toward an unnamed lake. Along the way, pick up the old two-track jeep trail, and follow it down to the west end of the lake. Rock hop over the inlet stream, skirting the west side of the lake. Cross a second inlet stream, and ascend the hill east of the rock formations and drainage. At the ridge, bear to the right, following the old jeep tracks around the west side of the lake. At the south end of the lake, leave the tracks and head south across the exposed landscape. Descend into the carved depression, exploring the many Highline Trail Lakes. This is our turnaround spot.

To hike further, head northeast and cross Wyoming Creek towards the distinct Line Creek Plateau. Pick up the jeep trail again above the treeline in the Wyoming Creek drainage. The trail follows the immense plateau for several miles to the Corral Creek Trail (Hike 20) and Maurice Creek Trail (Hike 19).

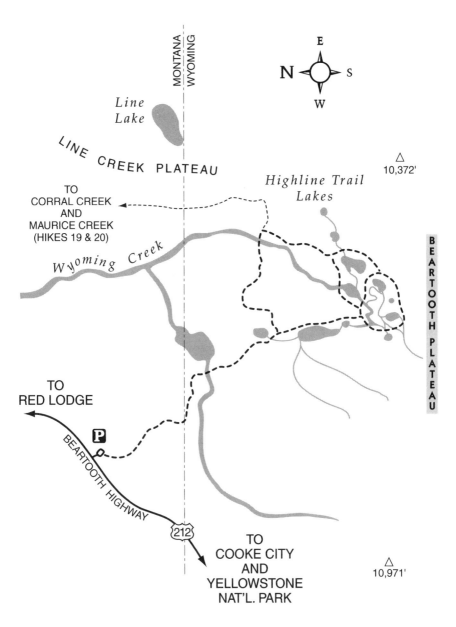

MONTANA
WYOMING

Line
Lake

LINE CREEK PLATEAU

E
N ◇ S
W

△
10,372'

Highline Trail
Lakes

TO
CORRAL CREEK
AND
MAURICE CREEK
(HIKES 19 & 20)

Wyoming Creek

B
E
A
R
T
O
O
T
H

P
L
A
T
E
A
U

TO
RED LODGE

P

BEARTOOTH HIGHWAY

212

TO
COOKE CITY
AND
YELLOWSTONE
NAT'L. PARK

△
10,971'

HIGHLINE TRAIL LAKES
ON
LINE CREEK PLATEAU

Hike 29
Losekamp and Stockade Lakes
from the Gardner Lake Trailhead

Hiking distance: 8 miles round trip
Hiking time: 4 hours
Elevation gain: 1,150 feet
Maps: R.M.S. Wyoming Beartooths
      U.S.G.S. Deep Lake

map
next page

Summary of hike: Gardner Lake is a 24-acre tarn at the base of the Gardner Headwall. From the trailhead is a birds-eye view of the lake. The trail follows a portion of the Beartooth Loop National Recreation Trail through picturesque meadowlands, carved granite formations and forested groves. The path leads to Losekamp Lake and Stockade Lake in a sloping meadow at the base of Tibbs Butte. This trail may be hiked as a 6-mile shuttle to the Hauser Lake trailhead by Long Lake (Hike 30).

Driving directions: The trailhead is located on Highway 212—29 miles from downtown Red Lodge and 35.5 miles from Cooke City. The signed Gardner Lake trailhead is on the south side of the road, 2 miles east of the Beartooth Summit.

Hiking directions: Descend down the steep alpine slope along the east side of Gardner Lake. At the south end of the lake, cross a fork of Littlerock Creek, the outlet stream of the lake. Continue across the exposed alpine tundra to a junction at 1.6 miles. Take the right fork, cross the ridge and descend to the inlet stream at the north tip of Losekamp Lake. The lake rests in a narrow valley between sheer granite formations and the slopes of Tibbs Butte. Cross the stream and follow the west shoreline of Losekamp Lake to a signed junction. The right fork heads west to Hauser Lake and Long Lake at the Beartooth Highway (Hike 30). The left fork continues south, down the draw to Stockade Lake. A lakeside trail follows the west side of the lake. The main trail crosses the inlet stream and heads down the east side of the lake. This is our turnaround spot.

Hike 30
Losekamp and Stockade Lakes
from the Hauser Lake Trailhead

Hiking distance: 6 miles round trip
Hiking time: 3 hours
Elevation gain: 400 feet
Maps: R.M.S. Wyoming Beartooths
      U.S.G.S. Deep Lake

map
next page

Summary of hike: The hike to Losekamp and Stockade Lake follows a portion of the Beartooth Loop National Recreation Trail. The scenic trail crosses picturesque rocky meadows and subalpine forested knolls to the 9,400-foot high mountain lakes. Both lakes rest in forest-fringed meadows at the base of Tibbs Butte. The trail may be hiked as a 6-mile shuttle to Gardner Lake (Hike 29).

Driving directions: The trailhead is located on Highway 212—36.5 miles from Red Lodge and 28 miles from Cooke City. Park along the highway pullout at Long Lake. Across the road to the south is a sign that reads "Hauser Lake Trailhead."

Hiking directions: Start at the Hauser Lake trailhead across the road. Head south, following the cairns for a half mile to the north end of Hauser Lake. Sawtooth Mountain appears above the lake in the southeast horizon. Cross the Hauser Lake inlet streams, and pass a pond on the exposed, rolling alpine tundra. Head uphill through a subalpine forest to a ridge with dynamic views across the Beartooth Mountains. Descend and cross the rolling wildflower-covered grasslands, a stream and scattered trees to a signed junction on the west shore of Losekamp Lake. The left fork heads north, uphill to Gardner Lake. The right fork heads south and follows the lake's outlet stream to a creek crossing at Stockade Lake. An angler path to the right follows the west side of the lake. The main trail follows the east side of Stockade Lake. This is our turnaround spot.

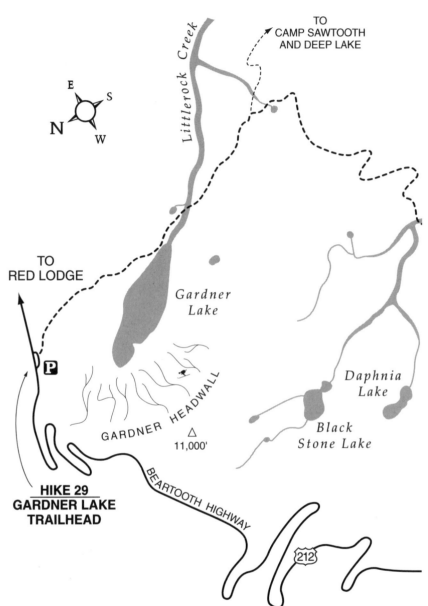

LOSEKAMP and STOCKADE LAKES

HIKES 29 and 30

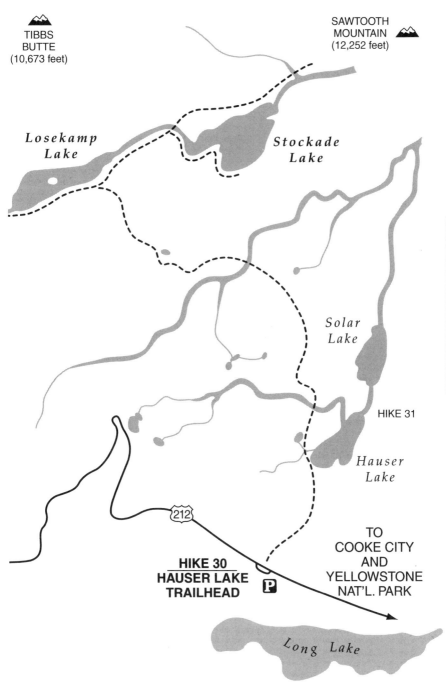

TIBBS
BUTTE
(10,673 feet)

SAWTOOTH
MOUNTAIN
(12,252 feet)

*Losekamp
Lake*

*Stockade
Lake*

B
E
A
R
T
O
O
T
H

P
L
A
T
E
A
U

*Solar
Lake*

HIKE 31

*Hauser
Lake*

212

TO
COOKE CITY
AND
YELLOWSTONE
NAT'L. PARK

**HIKE 30
HAUSER LAKE
TRAILHEAD** 🅿

Long Lake

Hike 31
Hauser, Solar, Fort
and Rainbow Lakes Loop

Hiking distance: 4 miles round trip
Hiking time: 2 hours
Elevation gain: 300 feet
Maps: R.M.S. Wyoming Beartooths
U.S.G.S. Deep Lake and Beartooth Butte

Summary of hike: This high altitude loop hike is an easy family outing to four beautiful alpine lakes above 9,600 feet. The panoramic views, forested knolls, rock-studded meadows, abundant wildflowers, meandering streams and pools encourage lingering and exploration.

Driving directions: The trailhead is located on Highway 212—36.5 miles from Red Lodge and 28 miles from Cooke City. Park along the highway pullout at Long Lake. Across the road to the south is a sign that reads "Hauser Lake Trailhead."

Hiking directions: From the Hauser Lake trailhead, cross the alpine meadow, following the cairns (manmade rock mounds used as trail markers). To the west is a view of Beartooth Butte. Descent into the draw, dotted with gnarled conifers, to the north end of Hauser Lake. The serrated ridge of Sawtooth Mountain rises above the lake. Leave the trail to Losekamp Lake (Hike 30), and follow the east side of Hauser Lake over the rolling, open tundra. Follow the stream flowing out of Hauser Lake to Solar Lake, a half mile ahead. From Solar Lake, cross the inlet stream, and head west over the hill to Fort Lake. Fort Lake is not visible until you crest the top of the hill. Walk around Fork Lake to the right, and head north to Rainbow Lake. Continue north, crossing the meadow back to the trailhead.

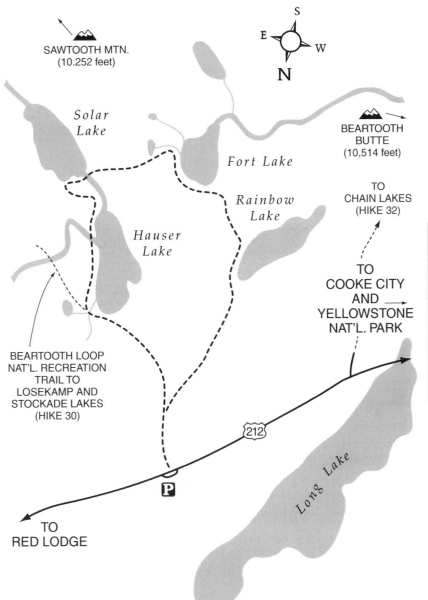

HAUSER, SOLAR, FORT AND RAINBOW LAKES

Hike 32
Upper and Lower Chain Lakes

Hiking distance: 6 miles round trip
Hiking time: 4 hours
Elevation gain: 300 feet
Maps: R.M.S. Wyoming Beartooths
U.S.G.S. Beartooth Butte

Summary of hike: Located in the glacial terrain of the Beartooth Plateau, this hike follows a wide but seldom used portion of the Morrison Jeep Trail through an evergreen forest to open alpine meadows. The meadows are covered in wildflowers and marbled with streams. Upper and Lower Chain Lakes are actually one large 80-acre lake. The lake is narrow through the middle, creating the appearance of two lakes. There are beautiful views, including a panoramic overview of Beartooth Butte.

The Morrison Jeep Trail is a rocky, unmaintained road that leads several miles down into the beautiful Box Canyon of the Clarks Fork. It is a popular route for experienced, confident mountain bikers.

Driving directions: The trailhead is located on Highway 212—35.5 miles from Red Lodge and 28 miles from Cooke City. Across the highway from the south end of Long Lake is a jeep trail. Park along the side of the jeep trail.

Hiking directions: Hike along the jeep trail to the bottom of the hill. The stream flows from Long Lake to Upper Chain Lake. You may stay on either the jeep trail that skirts the Chain Lakes or take the meadow to both lakes. Upper Chain Lake is about one mile from the trailhead, while Lower Chain Lake is just under two miles. Both lakes are visible from the trail. The jeep trail will continue past Dollar Lake on your left (2.2 miles) and Duck Lake on your right (3 miles). To return, follow the same trail back.

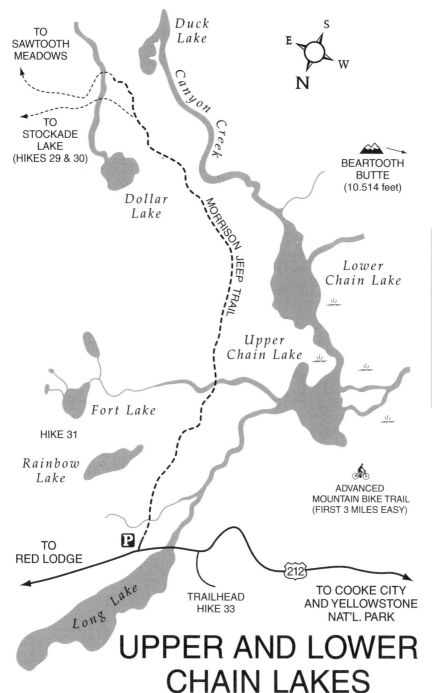

TO SAWTOOTH MEADOWS

TO STOCKADE LAKE (HIKES 29 & 30)

Duck Lake

Canyon Creek

S
E   W
N

BEARTOOTH BUTTE (10.514 feet)

Dollar Lake

MORRISON JEEP TRAIL

Lower Chain Lake

B
E
A
R
T
O
O
T
H

P
L
A
T
E
A
U

Upper Chain Lake

Fort Lake

HIKE 31

Rainbow Lake

ADVANCED MOUNTAIN BIKE TRAIL (FIRST 3 MILES EASY)

P

TO RED LODGE

212

TO COOKE CITY AND YELLOWSTONE NAT'L. PARK

Long Lake

TRAILHEAD HIKE 33

UPPER AND LOWER CHAIN LAKES

Hike 33
Dorf, Sheepherders, Snyder, Promise and Z Lakes

Hiking distance: 5.5 miles round trip
Hiking time: 3 hours
Elevation gain: 450 feet
Maps: R.M.S. Wyoming Beartooths
U.S.G.S. Beartooth Butte

Summary of hike: This hike does not have a path. Walk along open meadows, following Little Bear Creek and other meandering streams from lake to lake. The meadows contain numerous streams that snake to the main drainage feeding the lakes. There are beautiful rocks covered with myriad colors of lichen. Evergreen trees break up the meadows and add to the variety of scenery.

Driving directions: Take Highway 212 to Long Lake—35.5 miles from Red Lodge and 28 miles from Cooke City. Just west of Long Lake is an unimproved road that heads north a short distance. Turn north and park anywhere along the side of the road to begin the hike.

Hiking directions: Walk north along the unimproved road a short distance. You will see a stream about 100 yards to your right. Cross the stream, using the rocks as stepping stones, and follow the stream uphill. The stream will lead to Dorf Lake, a half mile from the trailhead. The trail parallels Little Bear Creek to Lower and Upper Sheepherder Lakes, located about two miles from the trailhead. From Upper Sheepherder Lake, there are two hiking options. To the left, about 10 minutes away, is Snyder Lake sitting above 10,000 feet. The other option is to continue northerly (uphill) to Lake Promise and Z Lake, located a half mile past Upper Sheepherder Lake. All of these lakes are beautiful and worth the hike. Return along the same route by following the drainage downhill.

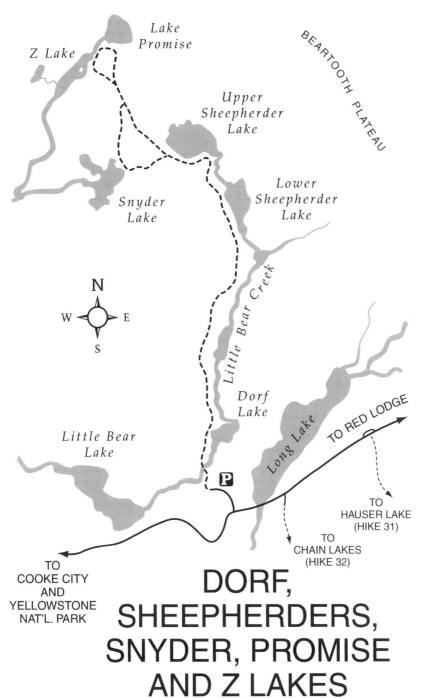

Z Lake

Lake Promise

BEARTOOTH PLATEAU

Upper Sheepherder Lake

Lower Sheepherder Lake

Snyder Lake

Little Bear Creek

N
W — E
S

Dorf Lake

Long Lake

TO RED LODGE

Little Bear Lake

P

BEARTOOTH PLATEAU

TO HAUSER LAKE (HIKE 31)

TO CHAIN LAKES (HIKE 32)

TO COOKE CITY AND YELLOWSTONE NAT'L. PARK

DORF, SHEEPHERDERS, SNYDER, PROMISE AND Z LAKES

Hike 34
Island and Night Lakes

Hiking distance: 3 miles round trip
Hiking time: 1.5 hours
Elevation gain: Level
Maps: R.M.S. Wyoming Beartooths
       U.S.G.S. Beartooth Butte

Summary of hike: Located in the high lakes area of the Beartooths, this extremely scenic hike stays close to the west shores of both Island Lake and Night Lake. The alpine lakes sit at an elevation of 9,500 feet and are surrounded by snowy peaks. Island Lake, the larger of the two, encompasses more than 140 acres and contains several islands. There is a crossing of Little Bear Creek, guaranteeing wet feet is early summer. This hike is the beginning of the Beartooth Highlakes Trail, which leads many miles up to the Beartooth Plateau.

Driving directions: On Highway 212, drive to the Island Lake turnoff—38 miles from Red Lodge and 26 miles from Cooke City. At the turnoff, turn north and continue 0.4 miles to the trailhead parking area near the boat launch and the Island Lake Campground.

Hiking directions: From the parking area, the trailhead is to the left along the west shore of Island Lake. A short distance ahead, the trail meets Little Bear Creek, the outlet creek of the lake. Wade or rock hop across the creek, and begin walking north along the shoreline. At the north end of the lake, the trail continues beside the creek connecting the two lakes. Continue north along the west shore of Night Lake. Although the trail continues farther into the backcountry, the turnaround spot for this hike is just north of Night Lake where the trail heads northwest away from the creek. Return along the same path.

    The trail continues to Beauty and Crane Lakes and may be hiked as a 5-mile shuttle hike to Beartooth Lake (Hike 35).

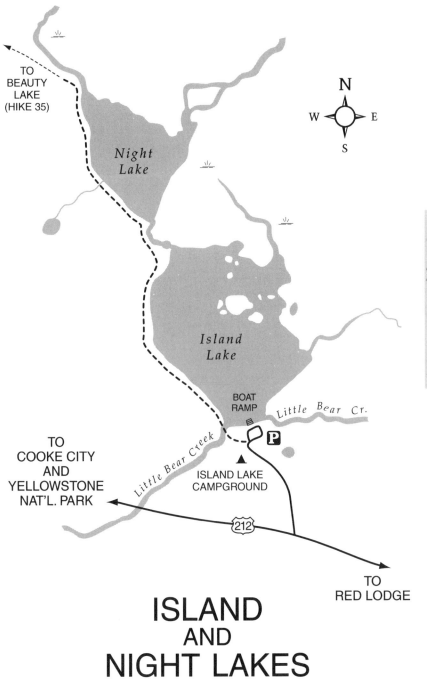

TO
BEAUTY
LAKE
(HIKE 35)

N
W — E
S

Night Lake

BEARTOOTH PLATEAU

Island Lake

BOAT
RAMP

Little Bear Cr.

P

TO
COOKE CITY
AND
YELLOWSTONE
NAT'L. PARK

Little Bear Creek

ISLAND LAKE
CAMPGROUND

212

TO
RED LODGE

ISLAND
AND
NIGHT LAKES

Hike 35
Beauty and Crane Lakes
from Beartooth Lake

Hiking distance: 4 miles round trip
Hiking time: 2 hours
Elevation gain: 520 feet
Maps: R.M.S. Wyoming Beartooths
       U.S.G.S. Beartooth Butte

Summary of hike: The Beauty Lake Trail begins at Beartooth Lake where the grandeur of Beartooth Butte towers 1,600 feet above the lake. The trail passes through forests and meadows at an elevation of more than 9,000 feet to Crane Lake and Beauty Lake. Both picturesque high mountain lakes have rock benches and are surrounded by granite domes, alpine meadows and conifer groves.

Driving directions: On Highway 212, drive to the Beartooth Lake Campground turnoff—41 miles from Red Lodge and 23 miles from Cooke City. Turn towards the campground, and drive 0.6 miles to the trailhead road. Turn left and continue 0.1 mile to the trailhead parking area.

Hiking directions: Head north toward Beartooth Lake to a signed junction. The left fork leads to Native Lake (Hike 36). Take the right fork and wade across Little Bear Creek, picking up the trail on the other side. (Early in the season, the water may be dangerously high and crossing is not recommended.) Continue through the pine and spruce forest, passing the east shore of Crane Lake at 1.3 miles. Several spur trails lead down to the shore. The main trail follows the cascading creek upstream to the southern tip of Beauty Lake, then parallels the eastern shore. This is our turnaround spot.

The Beauty Lake Trail intersects the Beartooth Highlakes Trail north of Beauty Lake. The right fork leads to Night and Island Lakes, a popular 5-mile shuttle hike (Hike 34). The left fork leads to Native Lake and may be hiked as an 8-mile loop (Hike 36).

N
W E
S

TO NATIVE LAKE
(HIKE 36)

HIGHLAKES TRAIL

TO
ISLAND
LAKE
(HIKE 34)

*Beauty
Lake*

TO
NATIVE
LAKE
(HIKE 36)

*Crane
Lake*

Beartooth Creek

**B
E
A
R
T
O
O
T
H
P
L
A
T
E
A
U**

BEARTOOTH
BUTTE
(10,514 feet)

*Beartooth
Lake*

Little *Bear Cr.*

P

BOAT
RAMP

BEARTOOTH
CAMPGROUND

212

TO
RED LODGE

TO
COOKE CITY AND
YELLOWSTONE
NAT'L. PARK

BEAUTY
AND
CRANE LAKES

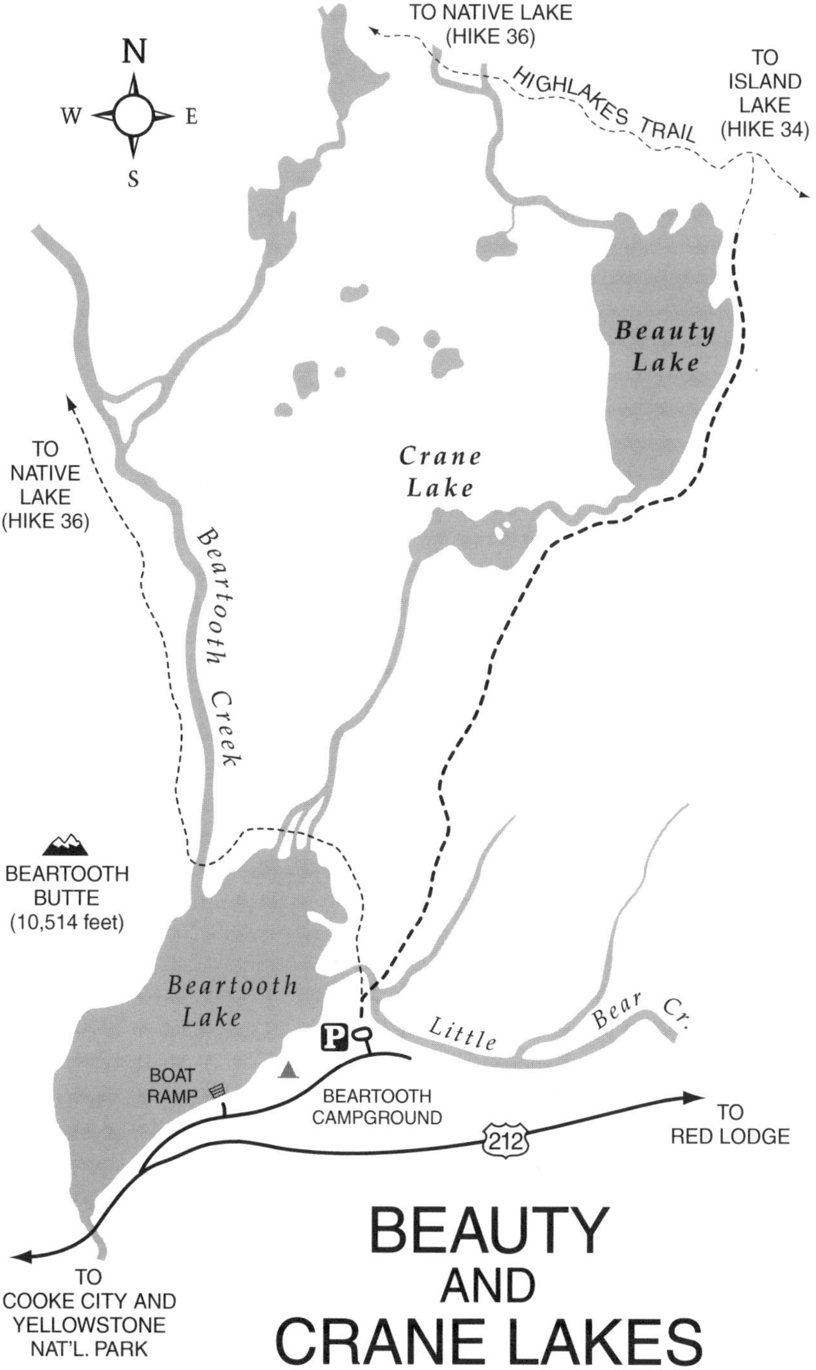

Hike 36
Native Lake from Beartooth Lake

Hiking distance: 8 miles round trip
Hiking time: 4 hour
Elevation gain: 900 feet
Maps: R.M.S. Wyoming Beartooths
        U.S.G.S. Beartooth Butte

Summary of hike: Native Lake sits in a seven-acre bowl at 9,800 feet, surrounded by meadows and stunted conifers. The trail begins by Beartooth Lake at the base of Beartooth Butte. The picturesque sedimentary rock of the butte dominates the landscape, towering 1,600 feet above the lake. The trail to Native Lake crosses open, alpine terrain along the slopes of the butte, parallel to Beartooth Creek.

Driving directions: Follow the directions for Hike 35.

Hiking directions: Walk towards Beartooth Lake and a signed trail junction. The right fork leads to Beauty Lake (Hike 35). Head towards the Highlakes Trail, straight ahead on the left fork. Wade across Little Bear Creek, and loop around the northeast perimeter of Beartooth Lake. Stay close to the forested hillside on the east edge of a marshy meadow. Cross four consecutive inlet streams. After crossing Beartooth Creek, the fourth stream, the trail curves north, away from Beartooth Lake. Climb the hillside through meadows with stands of evergreens. The trail traverses the terraced east slope of Beartooth Butte above the creek for two miles. At 2.6 miles, cross the creek, and continue north to a signed junction with the Beartooth Highlakes Trail. The right fork leads to Beauty, Night and Island Lakes. Bear left and recross the creek to another junction. The left fork heads west to Clay Butte (Hike 39). Continue 0.6 miles on the right fork to Native Lake. Return by retracing your steps.

    The trail may be hiked as an 8-mile loop with the Beauty Lake Trail, Hike 35.

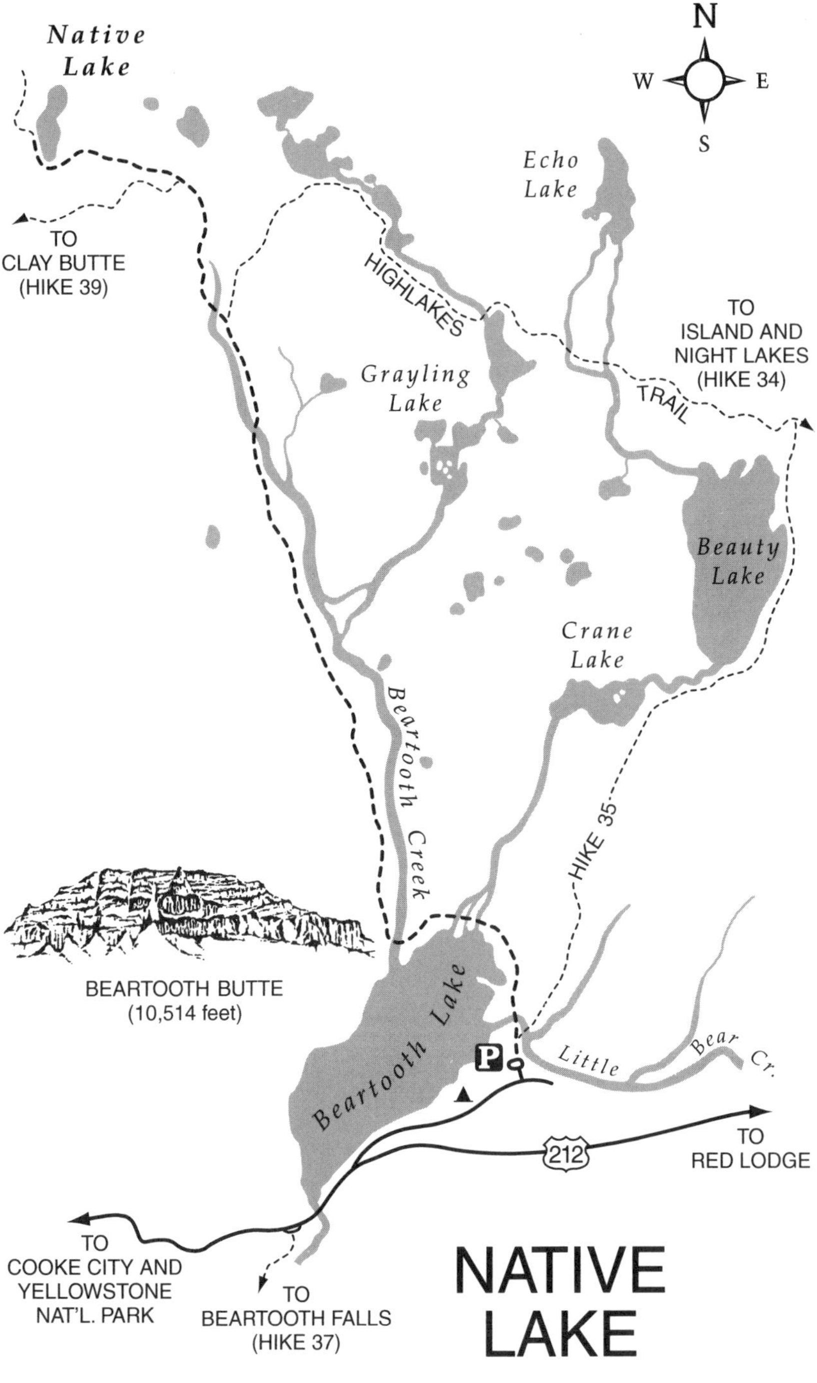

Native
Lake

N
W · E
S

Echo
Lake

TO
CLAY BUTTE
(HIKE 39)

HIGHLAKES

Grayling
Lake

TO
ISLAND AND
NIGHT LAKES
(HIKE 34)

TRAIL

BEARTOOTH PLATEAU

Beauty
Lake

Crane
Lake

Beartooth Creek

HIKE 35

BEARTOOTH BUTTE
(10,514 feet)

Beartooth Lake

P

Little

Bear Cr.

212
TO
RED LODGE

TO
COOKE CITY AND
YELLOWSTONE
NAT'L. PARK

TO
BEARTOOTH FALLS
(HIKE 37)

NATIVE
LAKE

Hike 37
Beartooth Falls

Hiking distance: 1 mile round trip
Hiking time: 30 minutes
Elevation gain: 150 feet
Maps: R.M.S. Wyoming Beartooths
U.S.G.S. Beartooth Butte

Summary of hike: The trail to Beartooth Falls is not a designated trail. It is, however, a hike you will long remember. There is a short scramble over large rocks to a spectacular waterfall. A tremendous volume of water plunges over 100 feet. CAUTION: You need to have good, stable footing while climbing over the rocks. The trail in this area is vague.

Driving directions: The trailhead is located on Highway 212—41.5 miles from Red Lodge and 22.5 miles from Cooke City. There are several car pullouts on each side of the highway bridge crossing Beartooth Creek at the south end of Beartooth Lake. The trail starts from the westernmost pullout, where the highway bends to the west.

Hiking directions: From the parking area, take the narrow trail into the forest towards the creek. The trail parallels the creek downstream through the lush ground cover. Within ten minutes, the trail meets boulders on the right and Beartooth Creek on the left. Begin the climb up the boulders to the plateau at the top. The trail is not clearly defined, but all routes lead up to the same area. Once on top, follow a footpath down in the direction of the thunderous sound of the falls. There are various lookout spots, from the beginning cascades to the lookout atop the falls. The views are guaranteed to give you vertigo. After admiring this powerful display of water, return along the same route.

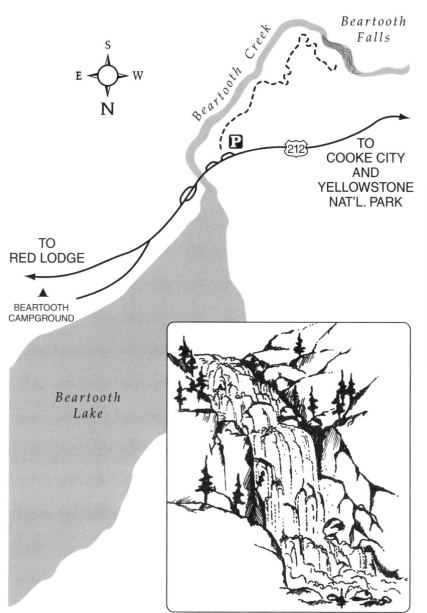

S
E · W
N

Beartooth Creek

Beartooth Falls

P [212]

TO
COOKE CITY
AND
YELLOWSTONE
NAT'L. PARK

TO
RED LODGE

▲
BEARTOOTH
CAMPGROUND

Beartooth Lake

BEARTOOTH PLATEAU

BEARTOOTH FALLS

Hike 38
Clay Butte Overlook

Hiking distance: 2.5 miles round trip
Hiking time: 1.5 hour
Elevation gain: 300 feet
Maps: R.M.S. Wyoming Beartooths
U.S.G.S. Muddy Creek and Beartooth Butte

Summary of hike: The Clay Butte Overlook begins at the 9,811-foot Clay Butte Fire Lookout. The panoramic views are as spectacular as you will find anywhere. The butte consists of sedimentary rock left by an ancient inland sea. The trail crosses the expansive alpine plateau, rich with wildflowers, to the edge of the weathered cliffs. The Beartooth Mountains, Beartooth Butte, the Clarks Fork valley, the twisting highway and the peaks of the Absaroka Range are all visible from this high mountain overlook.

Driving directions: The Clay Butte Fire Lookout turnoff is located on Highway 212—43 miles from Red Lodge and 22 miles from Cooke City. Turn north at the signed Clay Butte turnoff. Drive 2.6 miles up the winding, gravel road to the fire lookout at the end of the road.

Hiking directions: Before beginning the hike, visit the fire lookout tower and the enclosed observation and interpretive center. After marveling at the grand vistas from the fire lookout, return to the parking area, and follow the two-track trail across the high, open meadow with panoramic 360-degree views. The alpine meadow is often carpeted with a colorful display of wildflowers. The trail heads gently uphill to a knoll. Due to the high altitude, it is more tiring than it appears. Once at the top of the eroded bald knoll, the path ends at the edge of the limestone cliffs. A few large and distinct cairns mark the route. Follow the cliffs to numerous overlooks on the treeless and seemingly endless expanse. Choose your own turnaround spot and return along the same route.

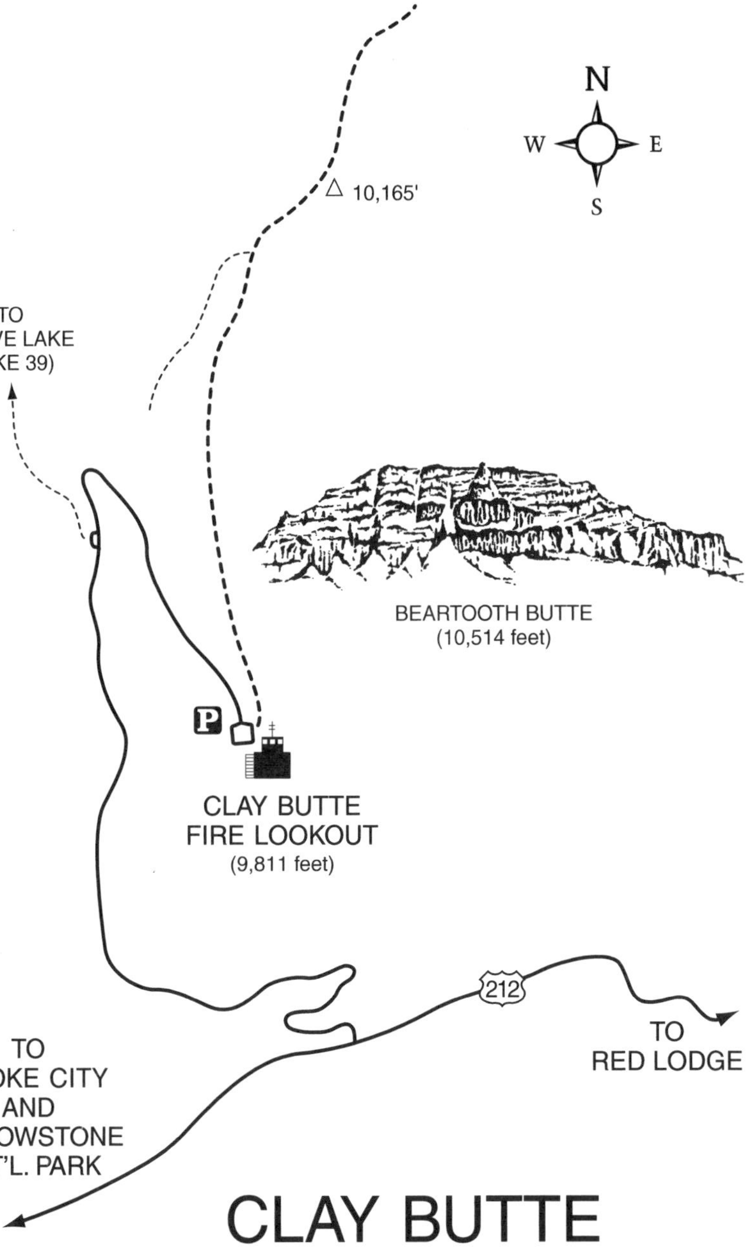

N

W ◆ E

S

△ 10,165'

TO
NATIVE LAKE
(HIKE 39)

BEARTOOTH BUTTE
(10,514 feet)

B E A R T O O T H   P L A T E A U

P

CLAY BUTTE
FIRE LOOKOUT
(9,811 feet)

212

TO
RED LODGE

TO
COOKE CITY
AND
YELLOWSTONE
NAT'L. PARK

CLAY BUTTE
OVERLOOK

Hike 39
Clay Butte to Native Lake
Upper Granite Loop Trail

Hiking distance: 7.6 miles round trip
Hiking time: 4 hours
Elevation gain: 800 feet
Maps: R.M.S. Wyoming Beartooths
U.S.G.S. Muddy Creek and Beartooth Butte

Summary of hike: Native Lake sits in a seven-acre bowl that is surrounded by meadows, stunted conifers and majestic snow-capped peaks. The trail begins at 9,550 feet, just below the Clay Butte Fire Lookout, and follows the west slope of the picturesque sedimentary rock of Clay Butte. The path crosses expansive alpine meadows filled with wildflowers and groves of Engelmann spruce, whitebark pine and subalpine fir. Throughout the hike are fantastic vistas of Pilot and Index Peaks and the Absaroka and Beartooth Ranges.

Driving directions: The Clay Butte Fire Lookout turnoff is located on Highway 212—43 miles from Red Lodge and 22 miles from Cooke City. Turn north at the signed Clay Butte turnoff. Drive 1.8 miles up the winding, gravel road to the signed Upper Granite Loop trailhead parking area on the left.

Hiking directions: Take the signed Upper Granite Loop Trail, crossing the rolling wildflower-filled meadow. Pass through several groves, entering the Absaroka-Beartooth Wilderness in a large meadow overlooking the Clarks Fork valley and the snow-capped Beartooth Range. Head downhill across the sloping meadow, crossing several small feeder streams and pockets of fir, spruce and pines. At the signed junction at one mile, take the right fork on the Clay Butte Trail. Continue northeast, gradually ascending the hillside through meadows and forest groves. At 2.5 miles, cross a small stream twice. Head up the draw to a saddle and junction with the Beartooth Highlakes Trail at the north end of Beartooth Butte.

(Whenever the trail fades, watch for cairns as a guide.) The right fork returns to Beartooth Lake (Hike 36). Bear left and descend 0.6 miles to Native Lake. The trail continues around the west side of the lake. Return along the same path.

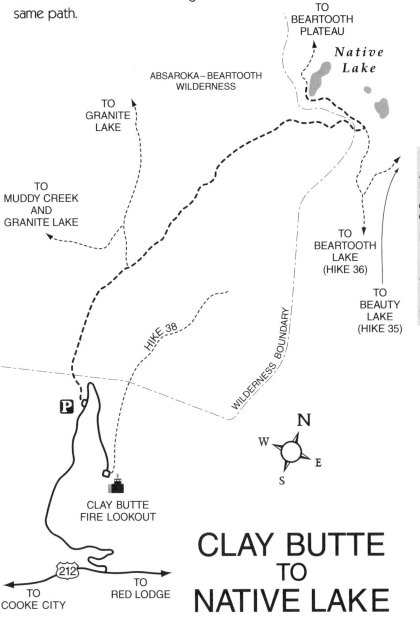

CLAY BUTTE
TO
NATIVE LAKE

Hike 40
Lily Lake

Hiking distance: 1 mile loop
Hiking time: 30 minutes
Elevation gain: 100 feet
Maps: R.M.S. Wyoming Beartooths
U.S.G.S. Muddy Creek

Summary of hike: This beautiful, 40-acre mountain lake sits at 7,670 feet. This hike is a one-mile loop along the southern portion of Lily Lake, which has an abundance of water lilies and is surrounded by a forest. Some of the best views of Pilot and Index Peak can be seen along the Lily Lake Road en route to the lake.

Driving directions: The turnoff to the trailhead is located on Highway 212—50 miles from Red Lodge and 14.5 miles from Cooke City. Turn north from Highway 212 onto Lily Lake Road. Drive up the winding road 1.2 miles to the T-junction. Turn right and continue 0.5 miles towards Lily Lake. As you approach the campground, turn right at each of the first two road forks. Park at the end of the road by the campsites.

Hiking directions: From the parking area, the unmarked trailhead begins to the left. Cross the Lake Creek tributary using stepping stones. The trail leads through the forest to the shoreline of Lily Lake near a rock outcropping. Take the fisherman trail to the left, which borders the lake along the southwest shore. Continue to the boat launch area. Walk up the gravel road leading back to the parking area on the left. There are additional trails along the lake north of the boat launch.

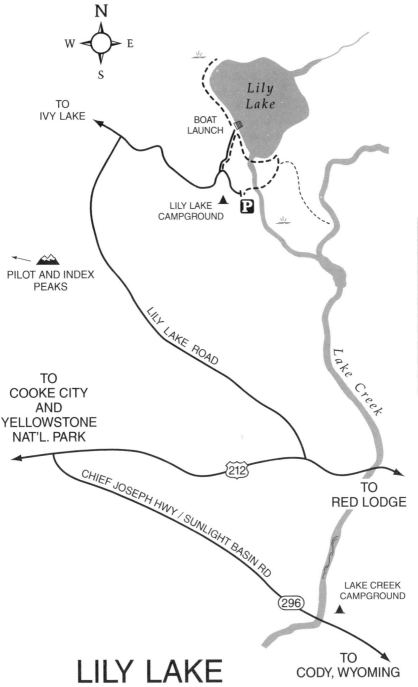

N
W E
S

Lily
Lake

TO
IVY LAKE

BOAT
LAUNCH

LILY LAKE
CAMPGROUND

P

PILOT AND INDEX
PEAKS

LILY LAKE ROAD

TO
COOKE CITY
AND
YELLOWSTONE
NAT'L. PARK

CHIEF JOSEPH HWY / SUNLIGHT BASIN RD

212

296

Lake Creek

BEARTOOTH HIGHWAY

TO
RED LODGE

LAKE CREEK
CAMPGROUND

TO
CODY, WYOMING

LILY LAKE

Hike 41
Clarks Fork Trail to Beartooth Creek

Hiking distance: 5 miles round trip
Hiking time: 2.5 hours
Elevation gain: 200 feet
Maps: R.M.S. Wyoming Beartooths
U.S.G.S. Muddy Creek, Hunter Peak and Windy Mountain

Summary of hike: The Clarks Fork Trail (also known as the Lewis and Clark Trail) is an extensive pack trail that leads eight miles to the Clarks Fork of the Yellowstone River. There are scenic vistas into the deep river canyon. This hike follows the first 2.5 miles on an easy meandering path to a footbridge over Beartooth Creek, a tributary of the Clarks Fork. The trail crosses through the rolling hills, rocky meadows and subalpine forested knolls north of the Clarks Fork.

Driving directions: The trailhead is located off Highway 212 on the Chief Joseph Scenic Highway (Wyoming Highway 296)—50.5 miles from Red Lodge and 14.5 miles from Cooke City. Drive 4.8 miles southeast on the Chief Joseph Scenic Highway to the signed Clarks Fork Trailhead turnoff on the left, directly across from Hunter Peak Campground. Turn left and follow the unpaved road 0.2 miles to the trailhead parking lot.

Hiking directions: Head east on the sandy path past the signed trailhead and cattle gate. Cross a trickling stream and a pond on the right. The near-level trail meanders up and down the rolling hills that are dotted with evergreens and colorful rock formations. At 0.7 miles, rock hop over Ghost Creek, and pass through an aspen grove in a small draw. Continue across the scenic landscape and cross another stream. Descend into a draw with beautiful rock outcroppings and a new-growth pine forest. The trail reaches Beartooth Creek and a footbridge with trail access gates at 2.5 miles. Return on the same trail.

To hike further, the trail continues parallel to the Clarks Fork, reaching the river in 8 miles at the Canyon Creek confluence.

TO
CODY, WYOMING

296

Clarks Fork Yellowstone River

Beartooth Creek

Ghost Creek

BEARTOOTH HIGHWAY

S
E ⊕ W
N

P

HUNTER PEAK
CAMPGROUND

TO
HWY 212
AND
COOKE CITY

CLARKS FORK TRAIL
TO
BEARTOOTH CREEK

Hike 42
Crazy Creek Falls

Hiking distance: 1 mile round trip
Hiking time: .5 hours
Elevation gain: 150 feet
Maps: R.M.S. Wyoming Beartooths
U.S.G.S. Jim Smith Peak

Summary of hike: Crazy Creek Falls is a short 15-minute hike, but it is worth spending a few hours here. The falls is a massive cascade, plunging over slabs of granite rock Along the edge of the thunderous cascade are flat, terraced rocks for sunbathing or hiking around. Beside the cascading waters and waterfalls are soaking pools and even a bubble-filled "jacuzzi." This natural water park is a favorite spot for those who know about it. The hike follows the first section of the Crazy Lakes Trail.

Driving directions: The trailhead is located on Highway 212—53 miles from Red Lodge and 11 miles from Cooke City. Pull into the parking turnout on the north, directly across from the Crazy Creek Campground.

Hiking directions: From the parking turnout, follow the Crazy Lakes Trail through a lodgepole pine forest. Within a few minutes, the massive cascade of Crazy Creek Falls is in full view. At 0.4 miles, watch on the left for a large, flat terrace of rocks. Leave the trail and hike along this terrace toward the sound of the water. This will quickly lead you to the water playground. Use caution in this area as the rocks can be slick and the water swift.

To hike further, continue to Ivy Lake, 3 miles ahead.

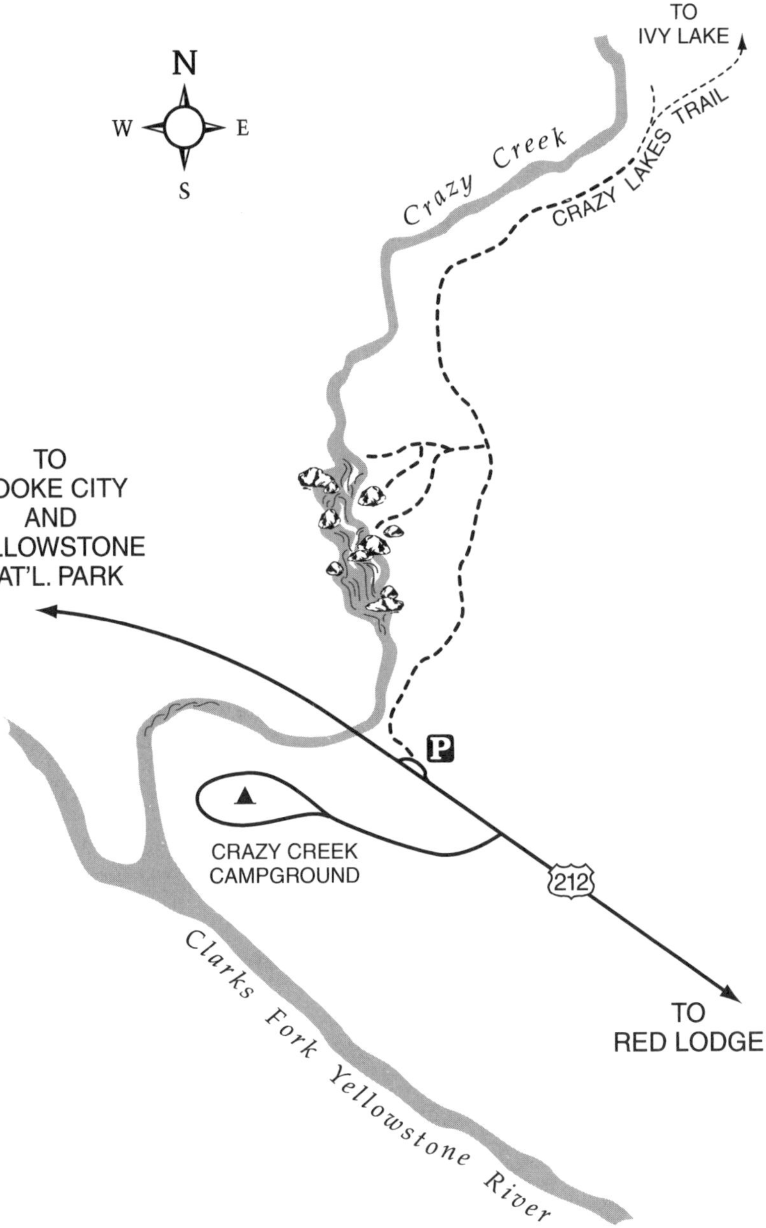

N
W E
S

TO
IVY LAKE

Crazy Creek

CRAZY LAKES TRAIL

BEARTOOTH HIGHWAY

TO
COOKE CITY
AND
YELLOWSTONE
NAT'L. PARK

P

▲
CRAZY CREEK
CAMPGROUND

212

TO
RED LODGE

Clarks Fork Yellowstone River

CRAZY CREEK

Hike 43
Pilot Creek Trail

Hiking distance: 5.6 miles round trip
Hiking time: 3 hours
Elevation gain: 800 feet
Maps: R.M.S. Wyoming Beartooths
      U.S.G.S. Jim Smith Peak and Pilot Peak

Summary of hike: The Pilot Creek Trail begins on the Beartooth Plateau at the base of Jim Smith Peak. The trail follows the cliffs overlooking the Pilot Creek drainage. The first 2.8 miles of the hike offer panoramic views of Jim Smith Peak, the snow-capped Beartooth Range, the Clarks Fork valley and a unique perspective of Pilot Peak. The entire 7-mile trail crosses high mountain meadows, a forested creek canyon and ends in a steep mountain cirque at the east flank of Republic Peak.

Driving directions: The trailhead is located on Highway 212—55.4 miles from Red Lodge and 8.9 miles from Cooke City. Turn south at the signed Pilot Creek Trailhead turnoff. Drive a quarter mile, curving around the perimeter of the gravel pit, to the signed trailhead parking area on the right.

Hiking directions: Climb up the forested path to a view of Jim Smith Peak on a ridge 150 feet above Pilot Creek. The trail follows the edge of the cliffs overlooking the cascading creek. Across the canyon is the sheer wall of Jim Smith Peak. At 0.6 miles, the path levels out in an open meadow that is teaming with wildflowers and has a magnificent view of Pilot Peak. Cross the meadows and the new-growth forest, staying on the edge of the cliffs. At 1.5 miles, the trail reaches a second meadow with far-reaching views across the Beartooth Plateau. Continue west towards Pilot Peak, following the cliffs above the creek. At the upper end of the meadow, the path enters the canyon and burn area from the 1988 fires along the south flank of Pilot Peak. Descend and cross a stream at 2.8 miles. This is a good turnaround spot.

To hike further, the trail continues up the canyon, reaching the signed North Absaroka Wilderness at 4 miles, ending at 7 miles in a steep, narrow cirque of mountains at the base of Republic Peak. (Just over the peak to the west is the Republic Creek Trail, Hike 51.)

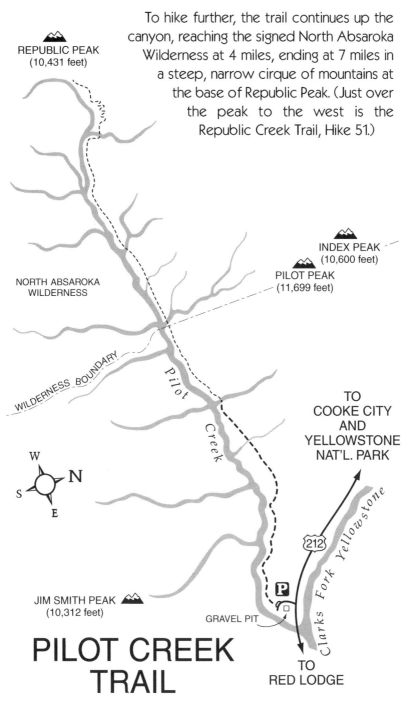

REPUBLIC PEAK
(10,431 feet)

INDEX PEAK
(10,600 feet)

PILOT PEAK
(11,699 feet)

NORTH ABSAROKA
WILDERNESS

WILDERNESS BOUNDARY

Pilot

Creek

TO
COOKE CITY
AND
YELLOWSTONE
NAT'L. PARK

Clarks Fork Yellowstone

212

W
N
S
E

JIM SMITH PEAK
(10,312 feet)

P

GRAVEL PIT

TO
RED LODGE

PILOT CREEK
TRAIL

Hike 44
Lillis and Vernon Lakes

Hiking distance: 5.5 miles round trip
Hiking time: 3 hours
Elevation gain: 600 feet
Maps: R.M.S. Cooke City
U.S.G.S. Fossil Lake

Summary of hike: This is a real backcountry hike into the Absaroka-Beartooth Wilderness. Few people hike to Lillis and Vernon Lakes, so chances are you will not see anyone along the trail. You may spot moose, which frequent the meadows. Lillis Lake is surrounded by dense forest and mountains peaks, including Pilot and Index Peaks looming above. The hike begins by the Clarks Fork Canyon Falls (cover photo). Mosquito repellent is highly recommended in the early summer.

Driving directions: The trailhead is located on Highway 212—61 miles from Red Lodge and 3.5 miles from Cooke City. It is directly across the highway from the Chief Joseph Campground. A trailhead sign posted along the highway reads "Clarks Fork Trailhead." Turn northeast and park in the parking lot 0.2 miles ahead.

Hiking directions: From the parking area, take the Kersey Lake Trail towards the bridge over the Clarks Fork. The Clarks Fork Canyon Falls is 100 feet downstream from the bridge. After crossing the bridge, a footpath and horsetrail parallel each other for over half a mile. Continue 0.5 miles through the shady forest to the Broadwater River Trail junction (Hike 47). Head right 1.2 miles, parallel to Sedge Creek, to the posted trail junction to Vernon Lake. The trail climbs gently, then heads down to a boggy meadow with logs to hop across. The trail quickly drops down to Lillis Lake. Continue following the northwest shore of Lillis Lake as the trail descends 300 feet through a dense forest to Vernon Lake. The trail ends at the north shore of the lake. Return along the same trail.

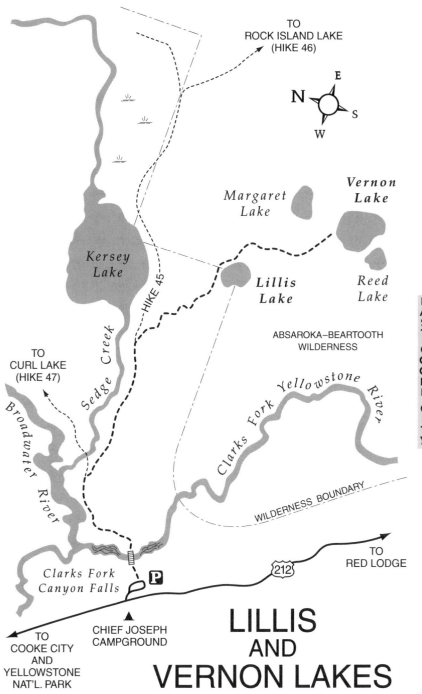

TO
ROCK ISLAND LAKE
(HIKE 46)

N E
W S

*Vernon
Lake*

*Margaret
Lake*

*Kersey
Lake*

*Lillis
Lake*

*Reed
Lake*

ABSAROKA–BEARTOOTH
WILDERNESS

HIKE 45

Sedge Creek

TO
CURL LAKE
(HIKE 47)

Clarks Fork Yellowstone River

Broadwater River

WILDERNESS BOUNDARY

TO
RED LODGE

212

*Clarks Fork
Canyon Falls*

P

CHIEF JOSEPH
CAMPGROUND

TO
COOKE CITY
AND
YELLOWSTONE
NAT'L. PARK

EAST COOKE CITY

LILLIS
AND
VERNON LAKES

Hike 45
Kersey Lake

Hiking distance: 3 miles round trip
Hiking time: 1.5 hours
Elevation gain: 100 feet
Maps: R.M.S. Cooke City
      U.S.G.S. Fossil Lake

Summary of hike: This forested hike to Kersey Lake is easy and pleasant. Kersey Lake is a large alpine lake surrounded by a rocky shore and forest. The trail to the lake follows the Broadwater River upstream for the first half mile. The remainder of the trail parallels Sedge Creek, the outlet creek from Kersey Lake. Near the trailhead is the Clarks Fork Canyon Falls and a magnificent cascade (cover photo).

Driving directions: The trailhead is located on Highway 212—61 miles from Red Lodge and 3.5 miles from Cooke City. It is directly across the highway from the Chief Joseph Campground. A trailhead sign along the highway reads "Clarks Fork Trailhead." Turn northeast and park in the parking lot 0.2 miles ahead.

Hiking directions: From the trailhead, walk to the bridge crossing the cascading Clarks Fork. A footpath and horse trail parallel each other for over half a mile. At 0.5 miles, pass a trail junction on the left that follows the Broadwater River to Curl and Broadwater Lakes (Hike 47). Stay right on the main trail to Kersey Lake. At 1.2 miles is another trail junction on the right leading to Vernon Lake (Hike 44). Stay left on the main trail. Near Kersey Lake, an anglers' path bears left along the shore-line. Stay on the main trail, which is minutes away from Kersey Lake. After enjoying the lake, return on the same path.

To hike further, parallel the south shore of Kersey Lake to Rock Island Lake (Hike 46), 1.5 miles ahead.

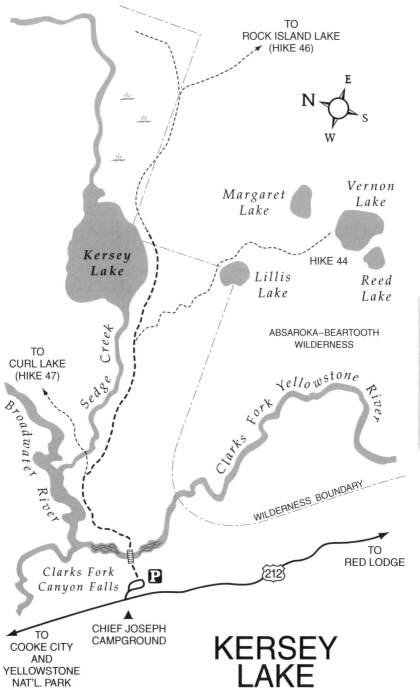

TO
ROCK ISLAND LAKE
(HIKE 46)

N
E
S
W

*Margaret
Lake*

*Vernon
Lake*

*Kersey
Lake*

*Lillis
Lake*

HIKE 44

*Reed
Lake*

ABSAROKA–BEARTOOTH
WILDERNESS

Sedge Creek

TO
CURL LAKE
(HIKE 47)

Clarks Fork Yellowstone River

Broadwater River

E
A
S
T

C
O
O
K
E

C
I
T
Y

WILDERNESS BOUNDARY

P

212

TO
RED LODGE

*Clarks Fork
Canyon Falls*

CHIEF JOSEPH
CAMPGROUND

TO
COOKE CITY
AND
YELLOWSTONE
NAT'L. PARK

KERSEY
LAKE

Hike 46
Rock Island Lake

Hiking distance: 6 miles round trip
Hiking time: 3 hours
Elevation gain: 200 feet
Maps: R.M.S. Cooke City
       U.S.G.S. Fossil Lake

Summary of hike: Rock Island Lake is a sprawling 137-acre lake in the Absaroka-Beartooth Wilderness. The lake sits in a flat, forested terrain with numerous wooded islands and primitive campsites. The irregular-shaped lake has cutthroat and brook trout. The well-maintained trail gains little elevation, making for a pleasant day outing. The hike begins by the Clarks Fork Canyon Falls (cover photo).

Driving directions: Follow the directions for Hike 45.

Hiking directions: From the north end of the parking area, cross the footbridge over the raging Clarks Fork River. Walk through the shade of a pine and fir forest towards Kersey Lake (Hike 45). A footpath and horse trail parallel each other for over a half mile. At 0.5 miles, pass the junction to the Broadwater River Trail on the left (Hike 47). Parallel Sedge Creek past the signed Vernon Lake junction on the right at 1.2 miles (Hike 44). At the southwest corner of Kersey Lake, an anglers' path bears left along the shoreline. The main trail follows the south side of Kersey Lake and traverses the north-facing slope high above the lake. Beyond Kersey Lake, the trail reenters the dense forest and skirts the south edge of a boggy meadow, reaching a signed junction at the Absaroka-Beartooth Wilderness boundary. The left fork leads to Russell Creek and Russell Lake. Take the right fork southeast towards Rock Island Lake. The level path leads 0.7 miles through lodgepole pines to the northwest corner of the lake. Angler paths meander along the shoreline. The southern route crosses talus slopes and the northern route crosses marshy wetlands.

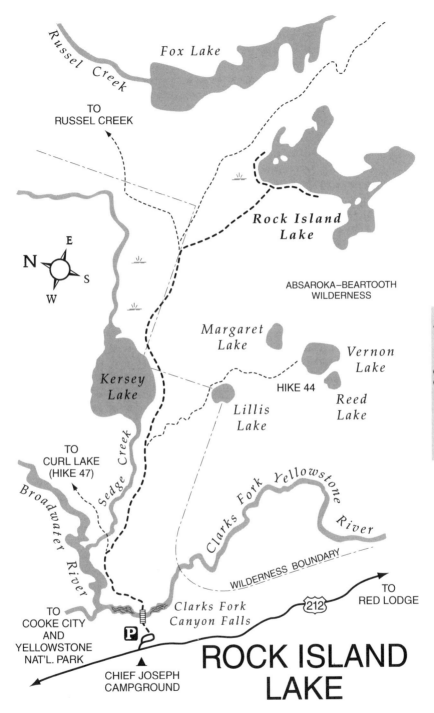

Russel Creek

Fox Lake

TO
RUSSEL CREEK

Rock Island
Lake

ABSAROKA–BEARTOOTH
WILDERNESS

N E S W

Margaret
Lake

Vernon
Lake

Kersey
Lake

HIKE 44

Lillis
Lake

Reed
Lake

TO
CURL LAKE
(HIKE 47)

Sedge Creek

Clarks Fork Yellowstone River

Broadwater River

WILDERNESS BOUNDARY

TO
RED LODGE

212

TO
COOKE CITY
AND
YELLOWSTONE
NAT'L. PARK

P

Clarks Fork
Canyon Falls

CHIEF JOSEPH
CAMPGROUND

EAST COOKE CITY

ROCK ISLAND LAKE

Hike 47
Broadwater River to Curl Lake

Hiking distance: 6.5 miles round trip
Hiking time: 3.5 hours
Elevation gain: 250 feet
Maps: R.M.S. Cooke City
U.S.G.S. Fossil Lake

Summary of hike: This top-of-the-world hike leads past cascading water, open meadows and trees to majestic high country lakes. Part of the trail goes through the burn area from the 1988 Yellowstone fires. Near the trailhead is a thunderous cascade as the Clarks Fork River is forced through a narrow gorge (cover photo).

Driving directions: The trailhead is located on Highway 212—61 miles from Red Lodge and 3.5 miles from Cooke City. It is directly across the highway from the Chief Joseph Campground. A trailhead sign along Highway 212 reads "Clarks Fork Trailhead." Turn northeast and park in the parking lot 0.2 miles ahead.

Hiking directions: The hike begins at the north end of the parking lot near the cascade and waterfall. The Clarks Fork Canyon Falls is 100 feet downstream from the wooden bridge. Follow the trail over the bridge. A footpath and horsetrail parallel each other for over half a mile. At 0.5 miles, watch for the Broadwater River Trail junction. Take the trail to the left. Continue gently uphill another half mile to a second posted trail junction for the Broadwater River Trail. Stay on this trail, following the cascading water upstream to Curl Lake, three miles from the trailhead. The trail parallels the east shoreline of the lake. To extend your hike another half mile, continue hiking to Broadwater Lake. To return, retrace your steps.

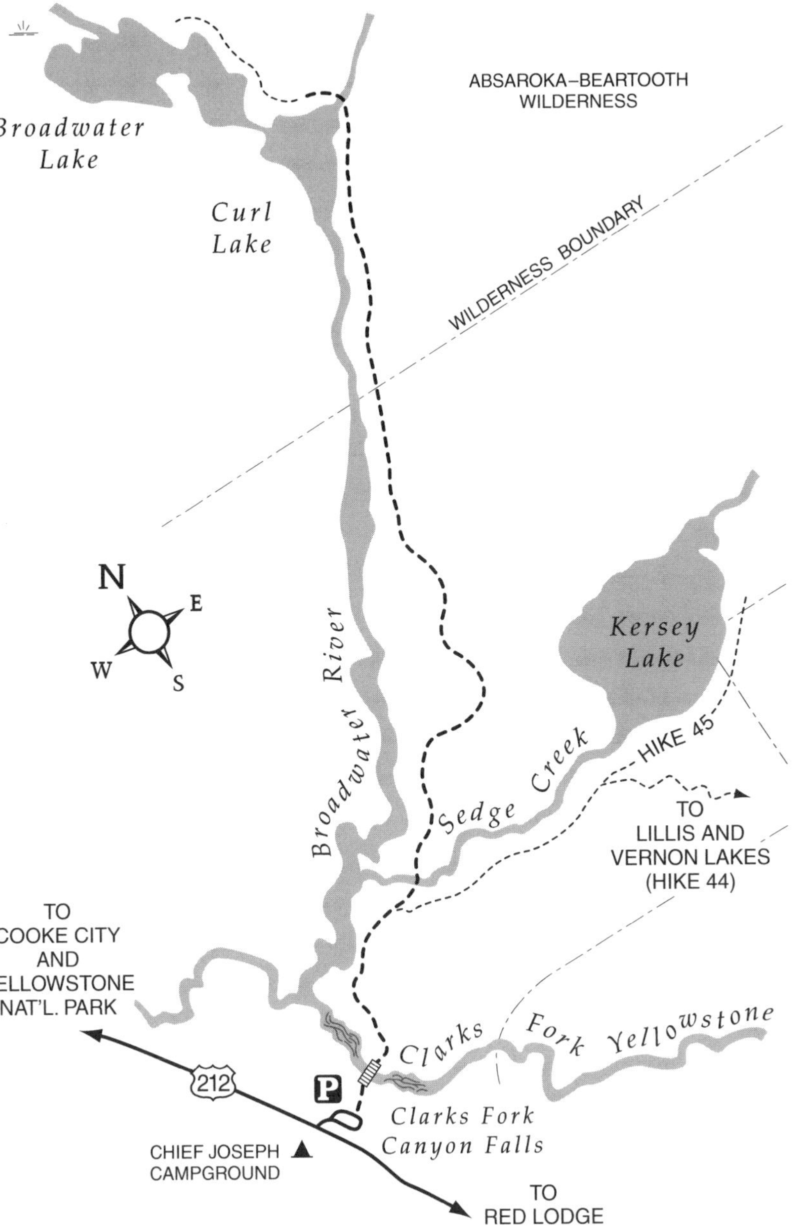

Broadwater
Lake

Curl
Lake

ABSAROKA–BEARTOOTH
WILDERNESS

WILDERNESS BOUNDARY

N
E
W
S

Kersey
Lake

Broadwater River

Sedge Creek

HIKE 45

EAST COOKE CITY

TO
LILLIS AND
VERNON LAKES
(HIKE 44)

TO
COOKE CITY
AND
YELLOWSTONE
NAT'L. PARK

Clarks Fork Yellowstone

212

P

Clarks Fork
Canyon Falls

CHIEF JOSEPH ▲
CAMPGROUND

TO
RED LODGE

BROADWATER RIVER
TO CURL LAKE

Hike 48
Lady of the Lake

Hiking distance: 4 miles round trip
Hiking time: 2 hours
Elevation gain: 300 feet
Maps: R.M.S. Cooke City
      U.S.G.S. Cooke City

Summary of hike: Lady of the Lake sits in a forested bowl surrounded by mountains at 8,800 feet. To the north and south of the 42-acre lake are meadows filled with wildflowers. Lady of the Lake Creek flows through the meadows and joins with the Clarks Fork of the Yellowstone. The forested trail to the lake crosses Fisher Creek, passes several old log cabins, and enters the Absaroka-Beartooth Wilderness. This is the beginning of the hike to Lower and Upper Aero Lakes.

Driving directions: From Cooke City, drive 2 miles east on Highway 212 to the unpaved Goose Lake Jeep Road on the left, just west of the Colter Campground. Turn left and continue 1.9 miles up the road to a road split. Go right 0.1 mile and park along the side of the road. (See inset map.)

Hiking directions: Head up the jeep road, following the trail sign. A short distance ahead, rock hop or wade across Fisher Creek. After crossing, bear to the right, heading uphill to the remnants of an old stone building and several log cabins on the left. Just beyond the cabins is a "Lady of the Lake-1 mile" trail sign. In reality, it is 1.5 miles to the lake. The trail gains elevation for a short distance before leveling off. Continue north through the forest, beginning the long descent to the lake. At 1.6 miles, the trail enters the Absaroka-Beartooth Wilderness. As the trail emerges from the trees, cross a large meadow with trickling brooks to the south end of Lady of the Lake. The trail winds along the west shore and then continues on to several high-altitude lakes. After enjoying the lake and alpine meadows, return to the trailhead on the same path.

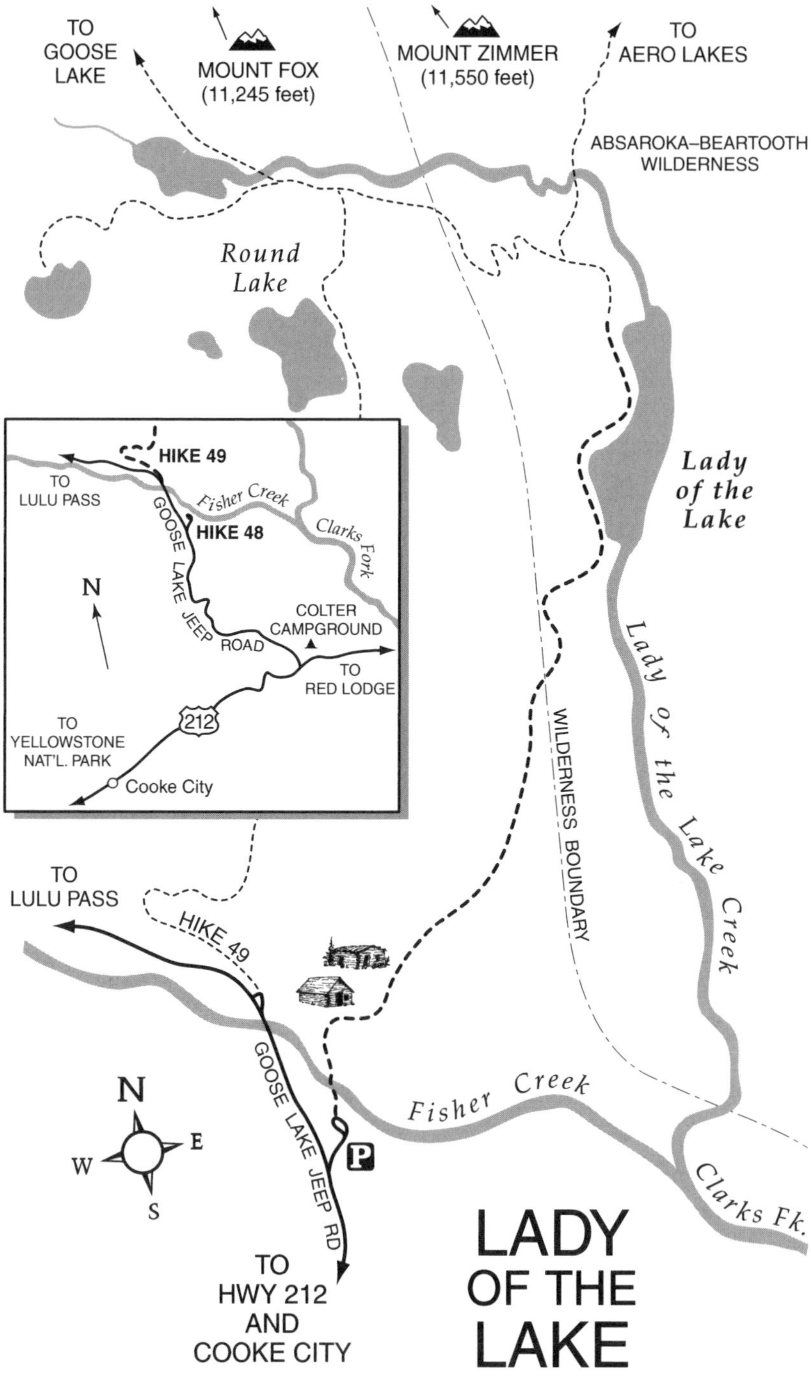

TO
GOOSE
LAKE

MOUNT FOX
(11,245 feet)

MOUNT ZIMMER
(11,550 feet)

TO
AERO LAKES

ABSAROKA–BEARTOOTH
WILDERNESS

*Round
Lake*

*Lady
of the
Lake*

HIKE 49

TO
LULU PASS

Fisher Creek

HIKE 48

*Clarks
Fork*

GOOSE LAKE JEEP

N

COLTER
CAMPGROUND

ROAD

TO
RED LODGE

212

TO
YELLOWSTONE
NAT'L. PARK

Cooke City

Lady

of

the

Lake

Creek

WILDERNESS BOUNDARY

TO
LULU PASS

HIKE 49

GOOSE LAKE JEEP RD

Fisher Creek

Clarks Fk.

N
W   E
S

P

TO
HWY 212
AND
COOKE CITY

LADY
OF THE
LAKE

Hike 49
Round Lake

Hiking distance: 3 miles round trip
Hiking time: 1.5 hours
Elevation gain: 500 feet
Maps: R.M.S. Cooke City
    U.S.G.S. Cooke City

Summary of hike: Round Lake is a gorgeous 31-acre lake sitting at an elevation of 9,340 feet. The lake is rimmed with grass and trees. The trail to Round Lake follows the Goose Lake Jeep Road, also used by all-terrain vehicles. The trail crosses through the rolling alpine terrain past conifer forest groves, rock outcroppings, and stream-laden meadows covered in wildflowers.

Driving directions: From Cooke City, drive 2 miles east on Highway 212 to the unpaved Goose Lake Jeep Road on the left, just west of the Colter Campground. Turn left and continue 1.9 miles up the road to a road split. Take the left fork 0.6 miles, crossing a bridge over Fisher Creek, to the signed Lulu Pass/Goose Lake road split. Park in the pullouts near this junction. (See inset map on Hike 48.)

Hiking directions: Take the Goose Lake Jeep Road to the right. Henderson, Scotch Bonnet and Sheep Mountains tower above the trail. Head uphill through the forest on the rocky jeep road for 0.7 miles, where the trail levels out in a meadow. Rock hop over a stream and continue along the meadow marbled with trickling streams and wildflowers. Follow the small dips and rises past beautiful rock outcroppings, and climb to a saddle overlooking Mud Lake on the left. The rock-lined lake appears more like a shallow pond. Curve around the lake and descend to Round Lake. Mount Zimmer, Mount Fox and Sheep Mountain rise above the lake. This is our turnaround spot.

To hike further, the trail skirts the east side of Round Lake, continuing past Lone and Star Lakes, to Goose Lake at 5.5 miles.

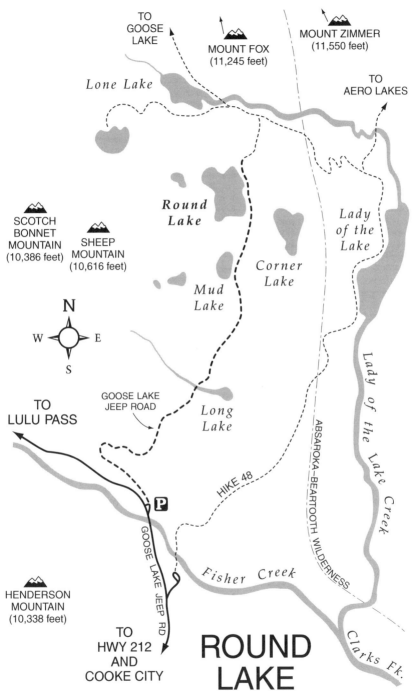

TO
GOOSE
LAKE

MOUNT FOX
(11,245 feet)

MOUNT ZIMMER
(11,550 feet)

TO
AERO LAKES

Lone Lake

*Round
Lake*

*Lady
of the
Lake*

SCOTCH
BONNET
MOUNTAIN
(10,386 feet)

SHEEP
MOUNTAIN
(10,616 feet)

*Corner
Lake*

*Mud
Lake*

N

W   E

S

GOOSE LAKE
JEEP ROAD

*Long
Lake*

TO
LULU PASS

Lady   of   the   Lake Creek

P

HIKE 48

ABSAROKA-BEARTOOTH WILDERNESS

HENDERSON
MOUNTAIN
(10,338 feet)

GOOSE LAKE JEEP RD

Fisher Creek

TO
HWY 212
AND
COOKE CITY

Clarks Fk.

ROUND
LAKE

NE COOKE CITY

Hike 50
Woody Falls

Hiking distance: 3 miles round trip
Hiking time: 2 hours
Elevation gain: 700 feet
Maps: R.M.S. Cooke City
      U.S.G.S. Cooke City

Summary of hike: Woody Falls is a spectacular 150-foot, three-tier falls with a pool at the base. The falls is a popular destination for the locals as well as a cross-country ski trail in the winter. The trailhead is located in the heart of downtown Cooke City. The hike begins on an old mining road that leads to the Mohawk Mine.

Driving directions: From downtown Cooke City, turn south from Highway 212 onto Republic Road 0.1 mile to a road split. Take the left fork on the unpaved road, and drive 0.2 miles to the loop at the end of the road. Park on the side of the road. If you do not mind fording a stream and prefer to walk from downtown, a second trailhead is located at the south end of River Street behind the general store. At the end of River Street is a buck fence and trail entrance. Walk south on the trail past old log cabins. Wade across the creek to the parking area.

Hiking directions: From the parking area off of Republic Road, walk up the jeep road to the southeast. Within five minutes from the trailhead is a well-defined footpath on the left. This is the trail to Woody Falls. For a short side trip, stay on the jeep road an additional 200 yards, just past a sign reading "Woody Creek Ski Trail." Take the spur trail to the right 100 yards to a beautiful cascade and smaller waterfall. Return to the main jeep trail and the Woody Falls Trail. The well-worn footpath begins a steady uphill climb through the forest. As the canyon below narrows, the falls can be heard on the right. Spur trails lead to the canyon edge for a variety of commanding overviews of Woody Falls. Return along the same trail.

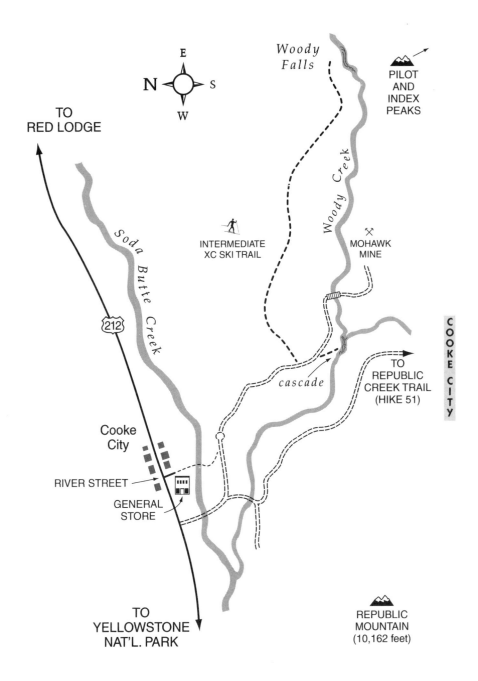

WOODY FALLS

Hike 51
Republic Creek Trail

Hiking distance: 5.6 miles round trip
Hiking time: 3 hours
Elevation gain: 450 feet
Maps: Trails Illustrated Tower/Canyon
U.S.G.S. Cooke City and Pilot Peak

Summary of hike: The Republic Creek Trail begins at Cooke City and follows a high mountain meadow parallel to Republic Creek. The trail crosses over Republic Pass at 4.5 miles, just west of Republic Peak, and connects with the Cache Creek Trail to the Lamar Valley in Yellowstone Park. This hike follows the first portion of the trail through the creek valley to the headwall at the north face of Republic Peak. There are scenic vistas of the surrounding peaks and a beautiful display of wildflowers.

Driving directions: From downtown Cooke City, turn south off Highway 212 onto Republic Road to a road split. Take the right fork on the unpaved road past some homes. Curve left up the narrow mountain road, and drive 1.3 miles to the signed Republic Creek Trail on the right. The trailhead is just past some old cabins and remnants of the Irma Mine. Park in one of the small pullouts.

Hiking directions: Head to the south on the signed footpath, crossing a small feeder stream of Republic Creek. At a quarter mile, the trail levels out and leads through the dense forest with a lush understory of grasses and flowers. Cross a rocky streambed, and emerge in an expansive rolling meadow dotted with trees and teaming with flowers. Continue south up the alpine valley between mountain peaks. At 1.5 miles the trail reaches Republic Meadow. This is a good turnaround spot for a 3-mile hike.

To continue hiking, skirt the west edge of the meadow, crossing several streams to the head of the valley at 2.8 miles in an ice-scoured cirque of mountains at the base of Republic

Peak and Republic Pass. From the bowl, the trail steeply ascends the mountain to Republic Pass at 4.5 miles. (Just over Republic Peak to the east is the beginning of the Pilot Creek Trail, Hike 43.)

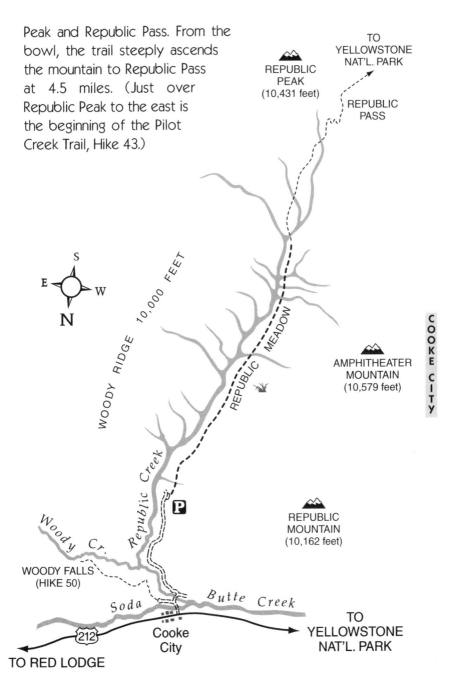

REPUBLIC CREEK TRAIL

Hike 52
Sheep Creek Falls

Hiking distance: 0.6 miles round trip
Hiking time: .5 hours
Elevation gain: 200 feet
Maps: R.M.S. Cooke City
       U.S.G.S. Cooke City

Summary of hike: Sheep Creek Falls is a magnificent, full-bodied waterfall surrounded by mountain peaks (back cover photo). Although it is only 0.3 miles to the falls, it is not an easy hike. It is more of a scramble up canyon and over timber along Sheep Creek. There is not a defined trail, and it is not recommended for youngsters. The hike climbs through a burn area from the 1988 Yellowstone fires.

Driving directions: The trailhead is located on Highway 212—1.1 mile west of Cooke City and 1.6 miles east of Silver Gate. The parking pullout is located on the south side of the highway and the west side of the Sheep Creek bridge.

Hiking directions: From the parking pullout, cross to the north side of Highway 212. Walk upstream along the east side of Sheep Creek. The trail fades in and out. Scramble upstream, using Sheep Creek as your guide. After climbing over and around down trees for a quarter mile, the canyon curves to the right. From this spot, the magnificence of Sheep Creek Falls is directly in view. Return by heading back downstream to the highway.

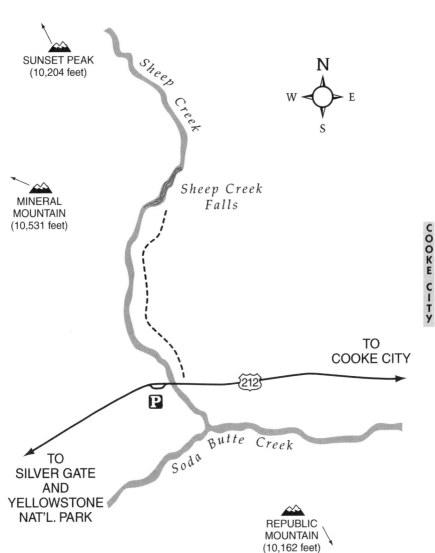

MILLER MOUNTAIN
(10,484 feet)

SUNSET PEAK
(10,204 feet)

Sheep Creek

N

W ⊕ E

S

MINERAL
MOUNTAIN
(10,531 feet)

Sheep Creek
Falls

COOKE CITY

TO
COOKE CITY

212

P

TO
SILVER GATE
AND
YELLOWSTONE
NAT'L. PARK

Soda Butte Creek

REPUBLIC
MOUNTAIN
(10,162 feet)

SHEEP CREEK FALLS

Hike 53
Bridal Falls

Hiking distance: 0.6 miles round trip
Hiking time: 15 minutes
Elevation gain: 50 feet
Maps: R.M.S. Cooke City
       U.S.G.S. Cooke City

Summary of hike: Bridal Falls, unofficially named, drops out of steep granite cliffs to a ledge. From the ledge, the water shoots out horizontal, dropping more than forty additional feet into a misty pool. Ferns and moss grow along these sheer rock walls. The trail is a short and easy path that parallels Wyoming Creek through the forest.

Driving directions: From downtown Silver Gate, turn south from Highway 212 onto Monument Avenue. Drive 0.2 miles to the end of the road. Turn left on Bannock Trail and continue 0.8 miles to the Wyoming Creek bridge, the only bridge along the road. Park off road before crossing the bridge.

Hiking directions: From the road, walk upstream along the west side of Wyoming Creek. The path leads south for 0.3 miles to the base of the falls and pool. The mountain on the left (east) of the falls is Republic Mountain. To the right (west) is Wall Rock. Return along the same trail.

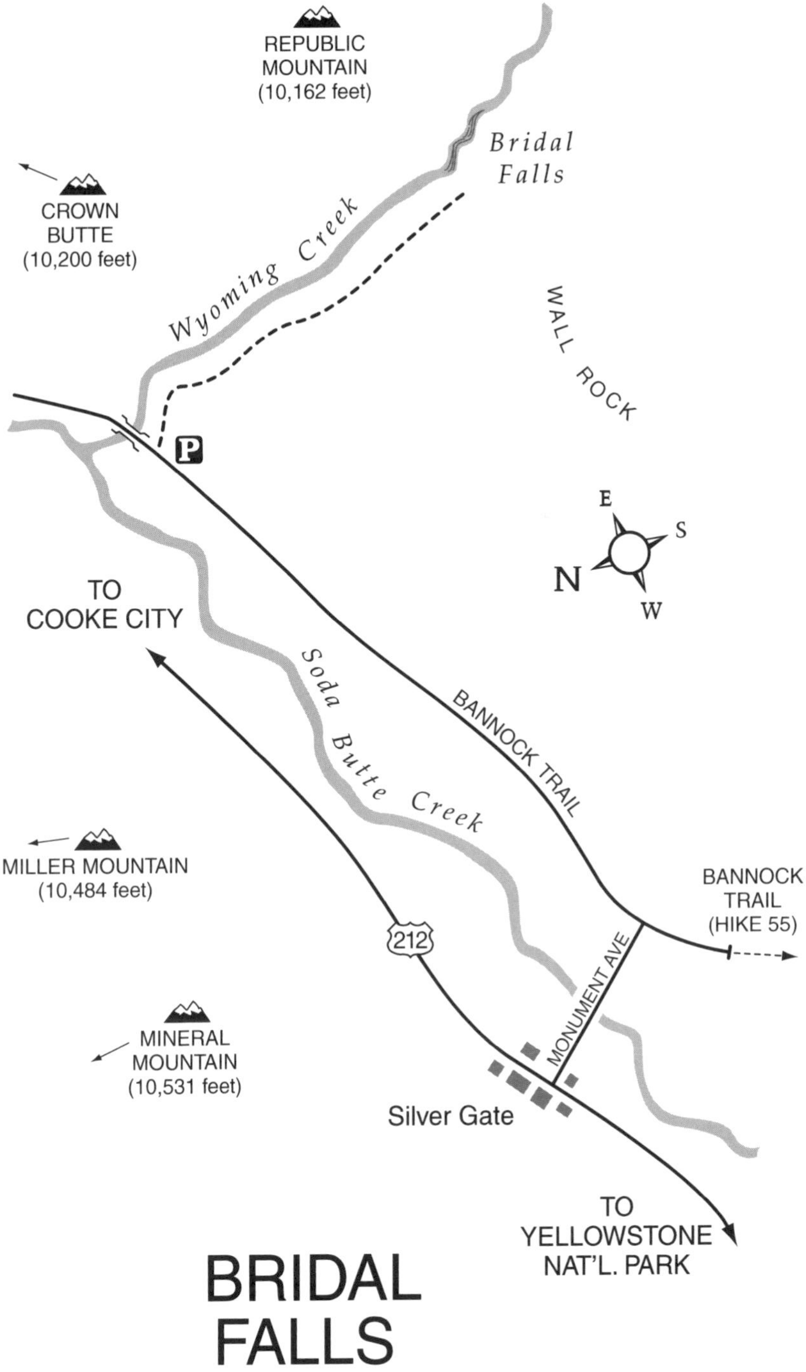

REPUBLIC
MOUNTAIN
(10,162 feet)

Bridal Falls

CROWN
BUTTE
(10,200 feet)

Wyoming Creek

WALL ROCK

P

TO
COOKE CITY

E
N — S
W

Soda Butte Creek

BANNOCK TRAIL

SILVER GATE

MILLER MOUNTAIN
(10,484 feet)

BANNOCK
TRAIL
(HIKE 55)

212

MONUMENT AVE

MINERAL
MOUNTAIN
(10,531 feet)

Silver Gate

TO
YELLOWSTONE
NAT'L. PARK

BRIDAL
FALLS

Hike 54
Silver Falls

Hiking distance: 2 miles round trip
Hiking time: 1 hour
Elevation gain: 350 feet
Maps: Trail Illustrated Tower/Canyon
      U.S.G.S. Cooke City and Cutoff Mountain

Summary of hike: Silver Falls is a long and narrow waterfall that drops more than 100 feet over a limestone cliff. The hike to the falls is along the eastern border of Yellowstone National Park, beginning from the town of Silver Gate. The second half of the trail parallels Silver Creek to the base of this beautiful falls.

Driving directions: Park at the far west end of Silvergate on Highway 212. From the northeast entrance station of Yellowstone National Park, the trailhead is one mile east on Highway 212.

Hiking directions: Walk 0.1 mile west on Highway 212 towards Yellowstone National Park. Take the unpaved road on the right 30 yards uphill to the powerlines and "private road" sign. Take the trail on the left, following the powerpoles 20 yards to the "trail" arrow sign on the right. Bear right on the footpath through the dense forest to an unsigned three-way trail split. Take the middle fork, straight ahead, to an old grass-covered road and another "trail" arrow. Bear left on the road. A short distance ahead, the road curves right to another road at a T-junction. Follow the arrow sign to the left through the burn area, reaching the east bank of Silver Creek. Take the creekside trail upstream above the drainage. As you near the head of the canyon, the trail becomes rocky. Descend into the canyon to the trail's end at the base of Silver Falls. Return along the same path.

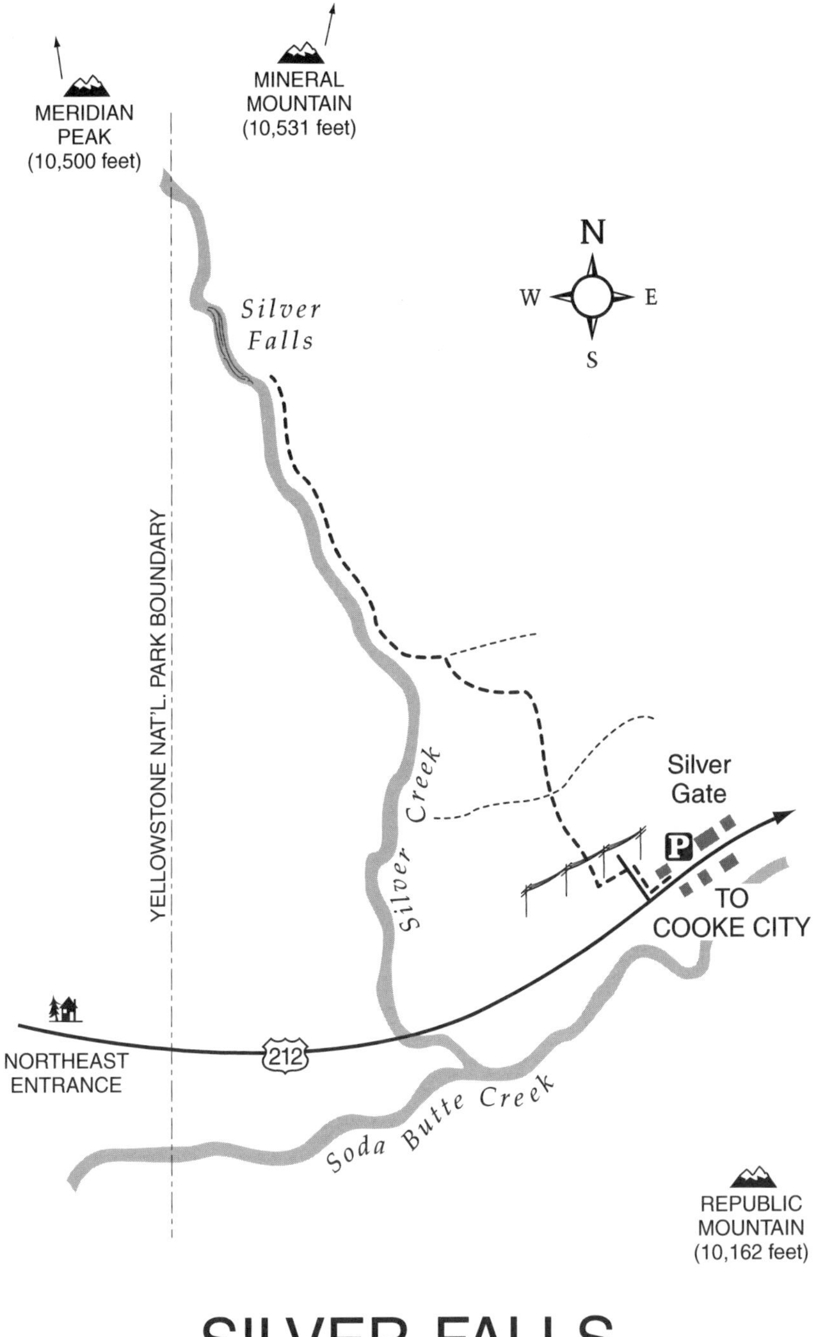

MERIDIAN
PEAK
(10,500 feet)

MINERAL
MOUNTAIN
(10,531 feet)

N

W ✦ E

S

*Silver
Falls*

YELLOWSTONE NAT'L. PARK BOUNDARY

Silver Creek

Silver
Gate

SILVER GATE

P

TO
COOKE CITY

NORTHEAST
ENTRANCE

212

Soda Butte Creek

REPUBLIC
MOUNTAIN
(10,162 feet)

SILVER FALLS

Hike 55
Bannock Trail

Hiking distance: 4.8 miles round trip
Hiking time: 2.5 hours
Elevation gain: 130 feet
Maps: Trails Illustrated Tower/Canyon
U.S.G.S. Cooke City and Cutoff Mountain

Summary of hike: The Bannock Trail is a short portion of the Bannock Indian route used to reach buffalo hunting grounds. The trail begins at Silver Gate in the North Absaroka Wilderness. The near-level terrain parallels Soda Butte Creek, a major tributary of the Lamar River, into Yellowstone National Park. The trail crosses several streams through open meadows and forest groves.

Driving directions: From downtown Silver Gate, turn south from Highway 212 onto Monument Avenue. Drive 0.2 miles, crossing over Soda Butte Creek, to the end of the road. Turn right on Bannock Trail and continue 0.1 mile to the end of the road at the signed trailhead. Park in pullouts alongside the road.

Hiking directions: Head west past the trailhead sign along the base of Amphitheater Mountain. The trail skirts the south edge of the meadow under the shadow of Abiathar Peak and Barronette Peak. Past the meadow, meander through a lush lodgepole forest. Ford a wide tributary stream of Soda Butte Creek and continue west. (Downfall logs can be used to cross the stream 20 yards downstream.) Across the canyon are the bald peaks of Miller Mountain and Meridian Peak. At one mile a sign along the trail marks the boundary between the Shoshone National Forest and Yellowstone National Park. Weave through the quiet forest, reaching the banks of Soda Butte Creek at 2 miles. Follow the creekside ledge downstream to a clearing by a feeder stream. Across Soda Butte Creek is the Warm Creek picnic area. To access the picnic area, you must wade across the creek. To return, take the same trail back.

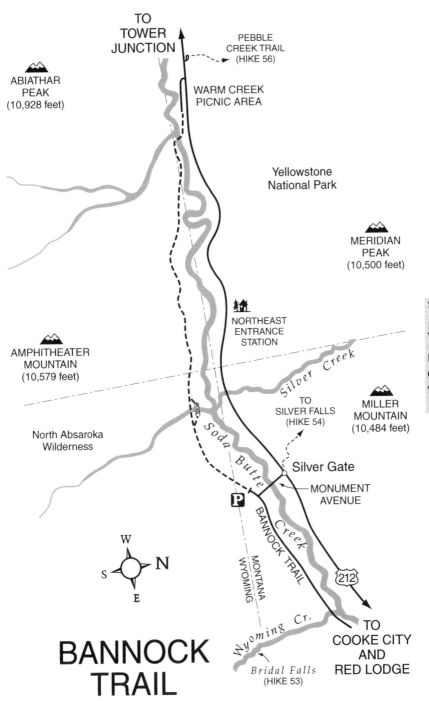

TO
TOWER
JUNCTION

PEBBLE
CREEK TRAIL
(HIKE 56)

WARM CREEK
PICNIC AREA

ABIATHAR
PEAK
(10,928 feet)

Yellowstone
National Park

MERIDIAN
PEAK
(10,500 feet)

SILVER GATE

NORTHEAST
ENTRANCE
STATION

AMPHITHEATER
MOUNTAIN
(10,579 feet)

Silver Creek

TO
SILVER FALLS
(HIKE 54)

MILLER
MOUNTAIN
(10,484 feet)

North Absaroka
Wilderness

Soda Butte

Silver Gate

MONUMENT
AVENUE

P

Creek

BANNOCK TRAIL

W
N
S
E

MONTANA
WYOMING

212

TO
COOKE CITY
AND
RED LODGE

Wyoming Cr.

BANNOCK
TRAIL

Bridal Falls
(HIKE 53)

Hike 56
Pebble Creek Trail from Warm Creek

Hiking distance: 7 miles round trip (or 12-mile shuttle)
Hiking time: 4 hours
Elevation gain: 800 feet
Maps: Trails Illustrated Tower/Canyon
U.S.G.S. Cutoff Mountain

Summary of hike: The Pebble Creek Trail is a 12-mile trail with trailheads at Warm Creek and the Pebble Creek Campground. This hike begins at Warm Creek and climbs to the Upper Meadows in a glacial valley at the north end of Barronette Peak. From the wildflower-covered meadow are panoramic views of the Absaroka Range and many of its peaks. The trail parallels Pebble Creek through the scenic valley for miles before reentering the forest. This trail may be combined with Hike 57 for a 12-mile shuttle hike.

Driving directions: From the northeast entrance to Yellowstone National Park, drive 1.2 miles west to the signed Warm Creek Trailhead turnoff. Turn right and drive 0.1 mile to the parking area at the end of the road.

From Pebble Creek Campground, drive 8 miles on the Northeast Entrance Road to the signed turnoff on the left.

Hiking directions: Follow the signed trail north, heading steadily uphill through the lush spruce and fir forest. At 0.4 miles, the trail bears left (west) on a more gradual slope. Continue climbing up the mountain. Near the top, emerge from the forest. Cross a talus slope with views of the Soda Butte Creek valley and the surrounding peaks. Reenter the forest for the final ascent to the 8,200-foot saddle, the high point of the hike at 1.5 miles. Gradually descend 200 feet to the high mountain meadow and Pebble Creek. Carefully ford the creek and head downstream through the expansive meadow dotted with spruce and fir trees. The trail continues 1.8 miles west through the Upper Meadows past numerous trickling streams and vistas of the surrounding peaks. At 3.5 miles, the trail reaches a second creek crossing near the west end of the meadow. This is the turnaround spot.

To hike further, the trail stays level for several miles before descending 1,000 feet to the Pebble Creek Campground, 8.5 miles ahead (Hike 57).

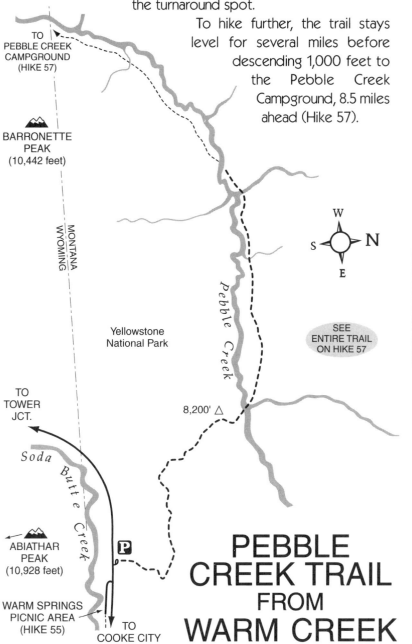

TO
PEBBLE CREEK
CAMPGROUND
(HIKE 57)

BARRONETTE
PEAK
(10,442 feet)

MONTANA
WYOMING

Yellowstone
National Park

Pebble Creek

W
S ✦ N
E

SEE
ENTIRE TRAIL
ON HIKE 57

TO
TOWER
JCT.

Soda Butte Creek

8,200' △

ABIATHAR
PEAK
(10,928 feet)

P

WARM SPRINGS
PICNIC AREA
(HIKE 55)

TO
COOKE CITY

**PEBBLE
CREEK TRAIL
FROM
WARM CREEK**

YELLOWSTONE

Hike 57
Pebble Creek Trail
from Pebble Creek Campground

Hiking distance: 5 miles round trip (or 12-mile shuttle)
Hiking time: 3 hours
Elevation gain: 1,200 feet
Maps: Trails Illustrated Tower/Canyon
　　　　 U.S.G.S. Abiathar Peak

Summary of hike: The Pebble Creek Trail is a 12-mile trail with trailheads at the Pebble Creek Campground and the Warm Creek picnic area. This hike begins at the Pebble Creek Campground. The forested trail, interspersed with small meadows, steadily climbs between 10,000-foot mountain peaks. This trail may be combined with Hike 56 for a 12-mile shuttle hike. For the one-way hike, it is recommended to begin from the Warm Creek Trailhead, which gains the majority of the elevation in the first 1.5 miles.

Driving directions: From the northeast entrance to Yellowstone National Park, drive 9.2 miles southwest to the signed Pebble Creek Campground turnoff. Turn right and park in the day-use parking spaces 0.2 miles ahead on the left.

From Tower Junction, drive 19 miles on the Northeast Entrance Road towards Cooke City to the turnoff on the left.

Hiking directions: Walk towards Pebble Creek, crossing the wooden footbridge over the creek next to campsite 32 and the restrooms. Head through the small meadow and ascend the hillside. The Pebble Creek Trail from the Northeast Entrance Road merges with the campground trail on a knoll at 0.2 miles. Bear left and climb another short hill to a view of Barronette Peak's southern flank. Cross the level area to the base of the mountain. Begin the ascent up the steep canyon, staying above the creek to the east. Switchbacks lead to a small meadow at one mile with great views of The Thunderer to the southeast. This is a good turnaround spot for a short hike.

To hike further, continue through the lodgepole pine, spruce and Douglas fir forest, crossing several tributary streams to the first crossing of Pebble Creek at 3.5 miles. Elevation gain continues gradually but steadily until reaching the Upper Meadows (Hike 56) and the Warm Creek trailhead, 7.5 miles further.

TO
HIKE 56
TRAILHEAD

BARRONETTE
PEAK
(10,442 feet)

CUTOFF ▲

HIKE 56

MONTANA
WYOMING

NORTHEAST
ENTRANCE

MOUNT
HORNADAY
(10,036')

BARRONETTE ▲

ABIATHAR ▲

Yellowstone
National Park

HORNADAY ▲

HIKE 57

PEBBLE CREEK TRAIL
HIKES 56 AND 57

Pebble Creek

YELLOWSTONE

TO
COOKE CITY

N

W ✦ E

S

NE ENTRANCE RD

Soda Butte Creek

PEBBLE CREEK ▲
CAMPGROUND

P

TO
TOWER JCT.

PEBBLE
CREEK TRAIL
FROM
CAMPGROUND

Hike 58
Trout Lake

Hiking distance: 2.2 miles round trip
Hiking time: 1 hour
Elevation gain: 200 feet
Maps: Trails Illustrated Tower/Canyon
        U.S.G.S. Abiathar Peak and Mount Hornaday

Summary of hike: Trout Lake, a great rainbow trout fishing lake, sits in a beautiful bowl. The round, twelve-acre lake is surrounded by rolling meadows, Douglas fir and lodgepole pine forests, and a sheer rock mountain wall to the north. From the lake are views of Mount Hornaday, The Thunderer, Druid Peak and Frederick Peak.

Driving directions: From the northeast entrance to Yellowstone National Park, drive 10.4 miles southwest to the unmarked trailhead pullout on the right. The pullout is 1.2 miles southwest of the Pebble Creek Campground.

From Tower Junction, drive 17.8 miles northeast towards Cooke City to the pullout on the left.

Hiking directions: From the parking pullout, hike west past the trail sign towards the Engelmann spruce and Douglas fir forest. Begin ascending the hillside to the forested ridge. Along the way, the cascading outlet stream of Trout Lake tumbles down the drainage to the left of the trail. At 0.6 miles, the trail reaches the southeast corner of Trout Lake at the outlet. Cross the log bridge over the creek. Once across, the trail follows the forested shoreline. A short distance ahead, the trail leaves the forest and emerges into open, rolling meadows with a wide variety of wildflowers. Continue along the shoreline, crossing a small bridge over the lake's inlet stream. Circle the perimeter of the lake back to the junction by the outlet stream. Take the left fork back to the trailhead.

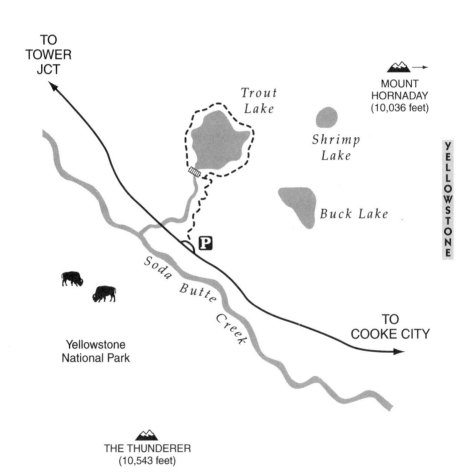

DRUID PEAK
(9,584 feet)

FREDERICK
PEAK
(9,585 feet)

TO
TOWER
JCT

MOUNT
HORNADAY
(10,036 feet)

*Trout
Lake*

*Shrimp
Lake*

Y
E
L
L
O
W
S
T
O
N
E

Buck Lake

P

Soda Butte Creek

TO
COOKE CITY

Yellowstone
National Park

THE THUNDERER
(10,543 feet)

TROUT LAKE

Other Day Hike Guidebooks

Day Hikes in Yellowstone National Park $9.95

Day Hikes in Grand Teton National Park and Jackson Hole 8.95

Day Hikes in the Beartooth Mountains
  Red Lodge, Montana to Yellowstone National Park 11.95

Day Hikes Around Bozeman, Montana 11.95

Day Hikes Around Missoula, Montana 11.95

Day Hikes in Aspen, Colorado 7.95

Day Hikes in Boulder, Colorado 8.95

Day Hikes in Steamboat Springs, Colorado 8.95

Day Hikes in Summit County, Colorado 8.95

Day Hikes in Sedona, Arizona 9.95

Day Hikes in Yosemite National Park 8.95

Day Hikes in Sequoia and Kings Canyon National Parks 12.95

Day Hikes Around Lake Tahoe 8.95

Day Hikes Around Los Angeles 11.95

Day Hikes in Ventura County, California 11.95

Day Hikes Around Santa Barbara, California 11.95

Day Hikes in San Luis Obispo County, California 14.95

Day Hikes on the California Central Coast 14.95

Day Hikes on Oahu 9.95

Day Hikes on Maui 8.95

Day Hikes on Kauai 8.95

Day Trips on St. Martin 9.95

These books may be purchased at your local bookstore or
outdoor shop. Or, order them direct from the distributor:

The Globe Pequot Press
246 Goose Lane · P.O. Box 480 · Guilford, CT 06437-0480
www.globe-pequot.com

800-243-0495

DAY HIKES IN
YELLOWSTONE
NATIONAL PARK

54 GREAT HIKES
ROBERT STONE

DAY HIKES IN
GRAND TETON
NATIONAL PARK
AND
JACKSON HOLE

ROBERT STONE

DAY HIKES IN THE
BEARTOOTH
MOUNTAINS

RED LODGE, MONTANA TO
YELLOWSTONE NATIONAL PARK
ROBERT STONE

DAY HIKES AROUND
BOZEMAN
MONTANA

INCLUDING THE GALLATIN
CANYON AND PARADISE VALLEY
ROBERT STONE

DAY HIKES AROUND
MISSOULA
MONTANA

INCLUDING THE BITTERROOTS
AND THE SHELBY–SWAN VALLEY
ROBERT STONE

DAY HIKES IN
SEQUOIA
AND
KINGS CANYON
NATIONAL PARKS

ROBERT STONE

DAY HIKES IN
YOSEMITE
NATIONAL PARK

25 FAVORITE HIKES
ROBERT STONE

DAY HIKES AROUND
LAKE
TAHOE

ROBERT STONE

DAY HIKES ON THE
CALIFORNIA
CENTRAL COAST

71 GREAT HIKES
ROBERT STONE

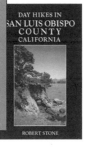

DAY HIKES IN
SAN LUIS OBISPO
COUNTY
CALIFORNIA

ROBERT STONE

DAY HIKES AROUND
SANTA
BARBARA
CALIFORNIA

46 OF THE BEST
ROBERT STONE

DAY HIKES IN
VENTURA
COUNTY
CALIFORNIA

43 OF THE BEST
ROBERT STONE

DAY HIKES AROUND
LOS ANGELES

45 GREAT HIKES
ROBERT STONE

DAY HIKES IN
BOULDER
COLORADO

ROBERT STONE

DAY HIKES IN
ASPEN
COLORADO

ROBERT STONE

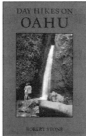

DAY HIKES ON
OAHU

ROBERT STONE

DAY HIKES ON
MAUI

ROBERT STONE

DAY HIKES ON
KAUAI

ROBERT STONE

DAY TRIPS ON
ST. MARTIN

ROBERT STONE

DAY HIKES IN
SEDONA
ARIZONA

25 FAVORITE HIKES
ROBERT STONE

Notes